80 NORTHERN COLORADO HIKING TRAILS

by Don and Roberta Lowe

THE TOUCHSTONE PRESS
P.O. BOX 81
BEAVERTON, OREGON 97005

*Library of Congress
Catalog Card No. 73-80046*

I.S.B.N. No. 0-911518-20-7

*Maps courtesy of
U.S. Geological Survey*

INTRODUCTION

Foot travelers in the backcountry of north-central Colorado are treated to exceptional displays of scenery, wild flowers and animal life. Any one of these three attractions alone would make hiking in this region special — the combination provides a triple delight. The terrain is a jumble of mountain chains separated by valleys and parks. Hundreds of lakes, ranging is size from dainty tarns to massive reservoirs, are tucked in basins or sprawl along valley floors. The profusion of wild flowers seem to bloom in shifts throughout summer and in fall their gay colors are replaced in many areas by the vivid yellow and gold quaking aspen leaves. The variety of birds is particularly impressive and the shy, little cony — so rarely seen in most high alpine areas — frequently is observed above timberline here. Marmots, chipmunks and squirrels also are common and rabbits, porcupines, beaver, elk, mountain sheep and many other animals thrive in certain areas.

The 80 trails described in this guide visit alpine regions in northern Colorado bordered by the State of Wyoming to the north, the Front Range on the east, Interstate 70-U.S. 6 on the south and Colorado 13-789 on the west. A map of the north-central portion of Colorado following the Table of Contents, which lists the trails in numerical order, shows the roads, towns, major peaks, lakes and streams and the distribution of the trails. The numbers of these hikes are printed in red and are grouped according to their common road access.

Each hike described in this guide has its own special features but attractive woods, verdant meadows and sparkling, often rambunctious, streams are common. Several hikes traverse tundra high above timberline. Seventy percent of the trips visit at least one lake and the majority of the remaining treks climb to the summits of peaks that offer far-ranging views.

The first six hikes visit lakes in the Flat Tops, a popular fishing area and the most westerly and southerly mountain area described in this guide. Hahns Peak (No. 7), only 11 miles from the Wyoming border, is the most northerly climb in the book. Trail No's. 8 through 19 penetrate the Park Range, the chain of mountains separating Steamboat Springs from North Park, but the hikes begin from four separate areas: trailheads for No's. 13 and 14 are near Steamboat Springs and No's. 15 and 16 start from the lush, rolling slopes at Rabbit Ears Pass. The remaining eight hikes enter the Mt. Zirkel Wilderness in the heart of the Park Range. Five trails, No's. 8 through 12, enter from the west side and the other three, No's. 17, 18 and 19, from the east. Two trips, No's. 20 and 21, climb to peaks in the Rabbit Ears Range, the southern boundary of North Park, and the ascent of the second, Parkview Mountain, offers an extraordinary view in all directions. Hikes No's. 22 and 23 visit the Gore-Eagles Nest Wilderness on the northeast side of the Gore Range. Another very scenic wilderness, the Rawah, situated northwest of Rocky Mountain National Park in the Medicine Bow Range, contains No's. 24 through 27.

Twenty-nine trails are in Rocky Mountain National Park and two others, No's. 28 and 50, climb to low summits on its periphery. Three hikes, No's. 28, 29 and 30, begin in Shadow Mountain National Recreation Area, a region administered by the National Park Service that adjoins the Park on the south, but only the latter two actually enter the Park. The trek to Crater Lake (No. 64), located beneath two small glaciers, begins at the southern edge of the Recreation Area and travels through Forest Service land for the entire distance. The Never Summer Range that forms the western boundary of the Park is visited by No's. 31, 32 and 33 and the short, strenuous climb of Specimen Mountain (No. 34) provides a good view of this chain. Hikes No's. 35 and 36 and 38 through 49 begin in the central portion of the Park on the east side and many share common trailheads. The beginning of the short climb through interesting rock formations to little Gem Lake (No. 37) is a few miles northeast of the town of Estes Park and the remaining trails in the Park are to the south along its eastern boundary. No's. 51, 52 and 53 are adjacent to Longs Peak and No's. 54 through 58 penetrate Wild Basin in the southeastern corner of the preserve.

Trails No's. 59, 60 and 61 head southwest from Fraser Valley into an experimental forest and access to the short hike to Columbine Lake (No. 65) is east across the valley. No.'s 62 and 63 climb from the ski areas at Berthoud Pass to unnamed peaks that are identified by their altitudes. The mountain area collectively called the Indian Peaks contains No's. 66 through 78: The first four in this group share trailheads near Brainard Lake and No's. 70, 71 and 72 begin a short distance by road to the southwest. The incredible drive to the trailhead for the hikes from Corona Pass along the Corona Trail (No. 73) and to King, Betty and Bob Lakes (No. 74) follows a former railroad grade and No's. 75 through 78 begin at the east end of the Moffat Tunnel. The most northeasterly and southeasterly trips are to Greyrock Mountain (No. 79), a dome with a lake on its summit located west of Fort Collins, and the short climb to Royal Arch (No. 80) in Boulder Mountain Park near Boulder.

HOW TO USE THIS BOOK

Preceding the body of the text for each trail is an information capsule listing seven important facts:

Hikes are recommended as **"one day trip"** or **"backpack."** A "one day trip" usually is either very short or lacks suitable sites for camping. A trip classified as a "one day trip or backpack" (for which you carry overnight camping equipment) means the hike can be done in one day but because of the length, scenic attractions, possible side and loop trips or the availability of good campsites, you may prefer to take two or more days. "Backpacks" are normally too long or strenuous for the average hiker to make without a layover before returning.

Hiking **distance** is measured one way only.

Since many hikes have a loss of altitude that is subsequently regained, **elevation gain** is listed as the total footage increment, not just the difference between the lowest and highest points. Significant elevation loss, if any, also is shown.

The **hiking time** is determined from the basic rate of two miles per hour plus allowance for rest stops, the steepness of the grade and the elevation gain. Trails are not graded according to difficulty, since this would necessitate a subjective evaluation that might not fit each individual's concept of an easy or hard hike. After a few trips you will be able to grade the trails for yourself by comparing the mileage and elevation gain, the major factors in determining how strenuous a hike will be, and by considering conditions such as the weather and how you feel on a specific day. Also, after a few hikes you will be able to predict whether your hiking speed is generally faster or slower than the times listed.

The **period when the trails are open** will vary each year depending upon the depth of the snowpack and the prevailing temperature. If you have doubts about a particular area, check with the ranger station nearest the trail, the district Forest Service office, Rocky Mountain National Park Headquarters or some other reliable source.

Since you will need to allow extra time to make a trip that travels at an elevation substantially higher than that to which you are acclimated, the **high point** for each hike is given.

The **U.S.G.S. topographic map name, scale and date** are included because many of the side and loop trips suggested in the text are off the maps printed for each trail and you may want to purchase the appropriate maps for the area. In major cities U.S.G.S. topographic maps are sold through selected retail outlets or you can purchase them from the U.S. Government by sending $.75 and identifying information for each map to: Distribution Section, Geological Survey, Federal Center, Bldg. 41, Denver, Colorado 80225. (The Glenwood Springs map cited for the trails in the Flat Tops is now out of print and maps of suitable scale are not available for Long Lake (No. 13) and Storm Peak (No. 14).

The text for each trail is in three main sections: the first paragraph(s) describe special features of the hike such as good viewpoints, impressive wild flower displays, the chance of spotting certain animals or possible side or loop trips. The second part gives driving directons. Although many of the access roads to the trailheads are unpaved, these generally have good surfaces. Sections of roads that are steep, narrow or rough are noted. The remainder of the text describes the trail route and includes comments on points of interest along the way and directions for any side or loop trips. Extreme steepness, lack of water, unmarked junctions, difficult fords and other problems you may encounter are noted. Where no specific details are given for a side or loop trip mentioned in the text, the route has not been scouted by the authors and is offered only as a suggestion for the explorative hiker.

The maps for each trail are enlarged or reduced sections of topographic maps produced by the U.S. Geological Survey. The items in red are those that are particularly important in helping you find, stay on and enjoy the trail. The legend for these items can be found following the Table of Contents.

The trail mileages shown may not always agree with those on trail signs. Map mileages are taken from known points or have been interpolated from specific fixes. Frequently, you will see trails on the topographic maps that are not overlayed in red. They either have no relevance to the trail being described or are no longer maintained. Campsites are marked with open triangles and may or may not be improved. Water is not necessarily available at these locations, although mention usually is made in the text if the spot is "dry." Important sources of water not obvious from the topographic map are identified by the word "water."

Despite their foreboding appearance, topographic maps are simple in theory and enable you to visualize the terrain covered by a trail. Through interpretation of these maps you can determine to some extent beforehand the difficulty of the trail and the feasibility of making a loop or reaching a lake or peak off the main route. Also, in case you become confused, being able to read a topographic may will make it easier for you to orient yourself.

The curvy lines on the topographic map are called contour lines and they connect points of equal elevation. The space between any two contour lines is termed a contour interval and is a measure of vertical distance. The closer the contour lines the steeper the terrain. How steep depends on the size of the contour interval which, in this book, is 40 feet usually but may be 20 feet — or even 200 feet. You can calculate the interval for a map by finding the difference between any two consecutive figures appearing along every fifth contour line and then dividing by five. Keep the contour interval in mind when you study each map because terrain that appears steep on a map with 40 foot contour intervals is far steeper than terrain marked by 20 foot contour intervals spaced the same distance apart on a map of the same scale.

Unshaded areas on the topographic maps are regions of little or no vegetation. Original topographic maps have a green overprint depicting the areas with plant cover. In this book these areas appear as a medium to dark grey shade depending on the density of the green ink used on the original map. Figures either along the contour lines, at the summits of peaks or elsewhere mark elevations above mean sea level.

Interestingly, the possessive apostrophe in place names, such as Longs Peak, is always omitted on topographic maps and have been omitted from the text, also. All maps in the book are north oriented.

Recreation maps prepared by the Forest Service and the National Park Service are another good source of information, particularly for extended excursions. Although these maps show most of the latest trails and are a great aid in planning side or loop trips, they do not show contour lines. The names and headquarters addresses of the national forests and national park in northern Colorado and the trails beginning within their boundaries are listed on page 175. For a last minute source of information, talk with ranger station personnel who have jurisdiction over the area you will be visiting. They often can tell you about new trails not shown on the maps and offer helpful suggestions.

HIKING and BACKPACKING IN NORTHERN COLORADO

Hiking and backpacking techniques are not discussed here because many fine books are available that cover the subject thoroughly. However, a few points concerning hiking in northern Colorado are reviewed.

Although many of the 80 trails can be accomplished in tennis shoes, a good pair of hiking boots with lug soles will give you better traction and more foot support. (Tennis shoes are good to have along to change into for fording streams and for camp wear.) Since you frequently will be hiking at high elevations across open terrain, you probably will want to wear sun glasses and if you sunburn easily a wide brimmed hat and long sleeved shirt are recommended.

Severe mountain storms can occur at anytime but after the first of September their likelihood increases with each successive day. High winds, especially in Rocky Mountain National Park, also are a continual possibility. For both comfort and safety always include a wool hat, gloves, a sweater, a windbreaker and a poncho or some other water-proof garment in your pack. A flashlight, halazone or some similar type of water purifying tablets and a first aid kit also should be standard equipment.

Thunderstorms are a common weather phenomenon throughout the Rocky Mountains. Although lightning strikes are not confined to high, exposed areas, you will be considerably safer on lower, wooded slopes. On hikes along open ridges or to a summit TURN AROUND AND RETREAT IF A THUNDERSTORM IS FORMING. They build very rapidly but after a quick progression of wind, hail or rain and lightning blue skies usually return swiftly. Thunderstorms usually form in the early afternoon, so you will have a better chance of completing a hike safely if you start early.

The plentiful supply of surface water in much of the alpine areas early in the summer affects the hiker in several ways. Most troublesome are the swollen streams. They present no problems in Rocky Mountain National Park as bridges have been constructed over all major creeks (and even most minor ones). Although many bridges have been built by Forest Service crews, some crossings in the National Forests must be done as fords. Mention always is made in the text of any trip that has such a crossing and none of the fords are particularly dangerous. In many areas the volume of the flow varies drastically from early to late summer and what was a rushing torrent in mid-June can be almost a trickle by the end of July. Early in the summer some of the trails go through marshy areas and these sections will become quagmires again after heavy rains. These wet areas usually are not extensive. Paradoxically, drinking water is not available on a few of the hikes and mention is made in the text if this is the case but it is always a good idea to begin every hike with a bottle of fresh water. Voracious mosquitoes thrive in some regions through July. An effective method of discouraging their attacks is to use a spray repellant on clothes and a cream for exposed skin.

Most of the hikes begin at 8,000 feet or higher and many go over 12,000 feet so if you are accustomed to functioning at considerably lower elevations you will need several days to acclimatize. Begin with easy hikes, climbing at a slow, steady pace, and gradually progress to more difficult trails.

Generally, the hikes are along easily followed trails. However, where the route may not be obvious, such as through marshy meadows, three standard markers — cairns (ducks), blazes and poles — are used to identify a route. The first is a pyramid of rocks ranging in size from three small stones to monuments several feet high; a blaze, found in wooded areas, is a long slash and a short one above it in the bark of a tree about six feet above the ground; the appearance of the pole is self-explanatory. Cairns, blazes and poles are placed so when you stand near one you usually can see the next marker along the route.

ALL BACKPACKERS IN ROCKY MOUNTAIN NATIONAL PARK MUST OBTAIN "BACKCOUNTRY USE PERMITS." These are free and can be obtained at the various Visitor Centers and from Park Rangers. Camping is permitted only at designated sites and wood fires are prohibited in some areas. The permits must be applied for in person not more than 24 hours before the trip is to begin. Also, dogs and other pets are not allowed on trails in the Park.

Be sure to sign in at the registers placed near the start of most trails. Knowing how many people use the backcountry and where they go helps Forest Service and National Park personnel determine the best management of the area.

The authors hiked each of the trails in this book during the summer of 1972 to insure that the most accurate and up-to-date trail information was available. However, trails change or are changed, either because of rock fall, washouts and other natural causes, or because the officials who maintain the trails decide to establish alternate routes. It is the intention of the authors to revise this volume every five years. If you wish to assist in this updating process, you are invited to send changes or irregularities noted on your hikes to the authors in care of The Touchstone Press, P.O. Box 81, Beaverton, Oregon 97005.

And please remember — do not litter and do not pick wild flowers or disturb plant and animal life.

D. L.
R. L.

contents

Trail No.		Page	Trail No.		Page
1	Mirror Lake	14	28	Shadow Mountain Lookout	68
2	Big Fish Lake	16	29	Lake Verna	70
3	Twin Lakes	18	30	Lakes Nokoni and Nanita	72
4	Wall Lake	20	31	Lake of the Clouds	74
5	Fraser Lake	22	32	Thunder Pass	76
6	Little Trappers Lake	24	33	La Poudre Pass	78
7	Hahns Peak	26	34	Specimen Mountain	80
8	Mica Basin	28	35	Ypsilon Lake	82
9	Gilpin Lake	30	36	Lawn and Crystal Lakes	84
10	Gold Creek Lake	32	37	Gem Lake	86
11	Three Island Lake	34	38	Deer Mountain	88
12	North Lake	36	39	Cub Lake and Mill Creek Basin	90
13	Long Lake	38	40	Fern and Odessa Lakes	92
14	Storm Peak	40	41	Lake Helene	94
15	Lost Lake	42	42	Bierstadt Lake	96
16	Rabbit Ears Peak	44	43	Flattop Mountain	98
17	Seven Lakes	46	44	Emerald Lake	100
18	Lake Katherine	48	45	Lake Haiyaha	102
19	Rainbow and Slide Lakes	50	46	Andrews Tarn	104
20	Hyannis Peak	52	47	Sky Pond	106
21	Parkview Mountain	54	48	Black Lake	108
22	Eaglesmere Lakes	56	49	North Longs Peak Trail	110
23	Upper Cataract Lake	58	50	Lily Mountain	112
24	Rawah Lakes	60	51	Eugenia Mine	114
25	Camp Lakes	62	52	Twin Sisters Peaks	116
26	West Branch Lakes	64	53	Chasm Lake	118
27	Blue Lake	66	54	Sandbeach Lake	120

Trail
No.   *Page*

55 Lion Lake 122
56 Thunder Lake 124
57 Bluebird Lake 126
58 Finch Lake 128
59 Byers Peak 130
60 St. Louis Lake 132
61 St. Louis Peak 134
62 Peak 12,424 (Berthoud Pass).. 136
63 Peak 12,845 (Berthoud Pass).. 138
64 Crater Lake 140
65 Columbine Lake 142
66 Mount Audubon 144
67 Mitchell and Blue Lakes...... 146
68 Lake Isabelle and
        Isabelle Glacier 148
69 Niwot Ridge 150
70 Arapaho Glacier 152
71 Arapaho Pass and Caribou Lake 154
72 Diamond Lake 156
73 Corona Trail 158
74 King, Betty and Bob Lakes..... 160
75 Arapaho Lakes 162
76 Crater Lakes 164
77 Clayton and Iceberg Lakes..... 166
78 Heart Lake 168
79 Greyrock Mountain 170
80 Royal Arch 172

LEGEND

⬢	Starting Point
- - - -	Trail
········	Obscure Trail
△	Campsite
▲	Campground
■ ◣	Building or Remains
8.0	Mileage
No. 611	Trail No.
S42	Road No.
⤙✕⤚	Bridge
══ ══	Access Road

11

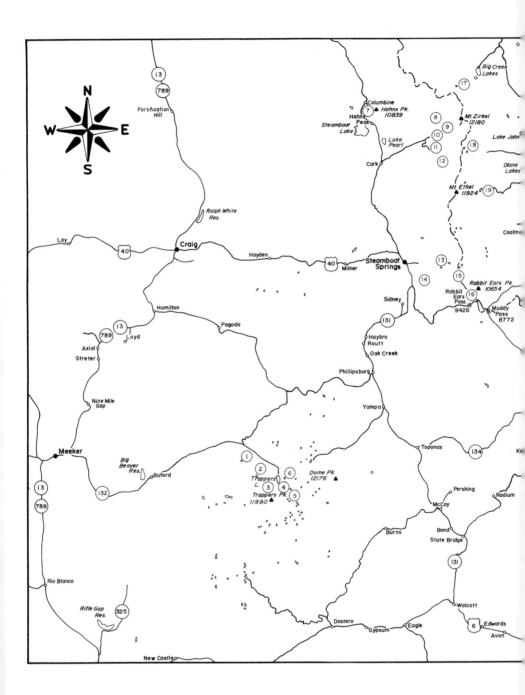

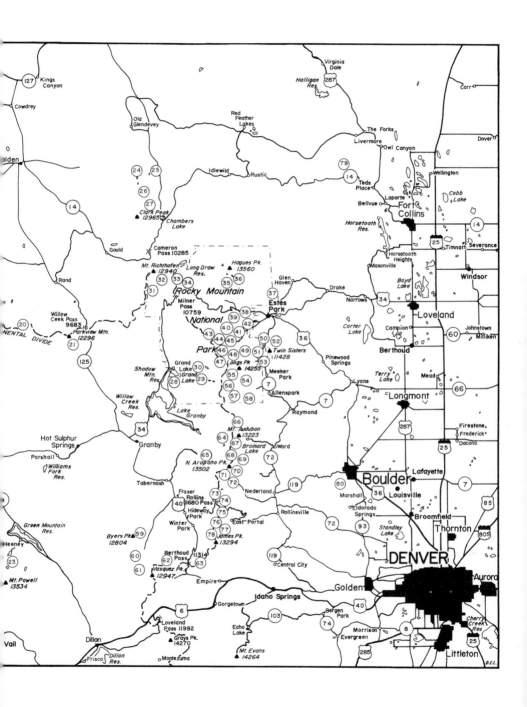

1 MIRROR LAKE

One day trip or backpack
Distance: 3 miles one way
Elevation gain: 1,700 feet, loss 100 feet
Allow 2 to 2½ hours one way
Usually open June through September
High point: 10,100 feet
Topographic map:
   Map of adequate scale unavailable

The most westerly area covered by this guide is the Flat Tops and six trails, all of them to lakes, penetrate the north central portion of this interesting and scenic region. Four of the hikes begin from Trappers Lake, a very popular fishing spot, and enter the Flat Tops Wilderness: The short trip to Little Trappers Lake (No. 6) travels one mile to the east and the longer hike to Fraser Lake (No. 5) ascends the wooded valley to the south. The most impressive feature in the Trappers Lake area is the 1,000 foot high basaltic cliffs that rise above the western and southern shore of Trappers Lake. From the top of these walls, extending a considerable distance to the south and west, is a lush rolling plateau covered with hundreds of tarns and lakes. Two of the hikes, Twin Lakes (No. 3) and Wall Lake (No. 4) climb to this plateau and side trips from Fraser Lake and Big Fish Lake (No. 2) can be made to the crest.

Unfortunately, afternoon thunderstorms are common so try to avoid the plateau during bad weather. Also, an infestation of bark beetles destroyed much of the spruce forest surrounding Trappers Lake and these dead trees are subject to blowdown so be alert while hiking and do not stop or camp under any of the affected trees.

Other enjoyable trails penetrate the Flat Tops but they are not included in this guide because adequate maps for the areas traversed have not been completed yet by the United States Geological Survey.

The trip to Mirror Lake climbs the southern slope of the valley formed by the North Fork of the White River as does the hike to Big Fish Lake. The trek begins in an open area of sagebrush, grass, and wild flowers then travels through woods and past several ponds before reaching the steep-walled basin that holds Mirror Lake.

Proceed on Colorado 13-789 to the junction of Colorado 132 two miles northeast of Meeker. Turn southeast and after 30 miles leave the paved surface and begin traveling on a dirt road. Nine miles farther turn right where a sign points to Trappers Lake. Continue three-quarters mile to a sign on your right listing mileages to Mirror and Sable Lakes. Turn south onto the side road and drive downhill for one-quarter mile to a small parking area and leave your car here.

Walk down the road for 0.2 mile to its end near a gate. Go through the gate and hike across an open slope then descend moderately to the bridge over the North Fork of the White River. Climb briefly before walking at a very gradual grade in a southeasterly direction through an aspen-rimmed meadow. Where the trail forks keep right, following a pole, and soon enter woods. After 100 yards come to a metal gate and continue climbing through the attractive forest.

Switchback twice and travel just below a little crest. Walk beside Mirror Creek for a short distance then switchback up to the opposite side of the low ridge. Continue climbing through woods at a steady, moderate grade, switchbacking periodically. Traverse along a slope of grass and trees, keeping left on the main trail where an unsigned path to Sable Lake heads upslope. Cross several shallow side streams then curve left and soon travel through a cleared area of blowdown. Come to a lush swale beside a stream and climb through woods for a few hundred yards. Walk beside ponds then wind up and traverse a grassy slope above two larger ponds. Switchback up through woods to a crest then drop into a little basin and walk through an area of hummocks. Climb slightly for a short distance in woods then travel through a little valley where the east wall is a rock slope and come to the northeast end of Mirror Lake.

Mirror Lake

Fisherman on the North Fork of the White River

2 BIG FISH LAKE

One day trip or backpack
Distance: 3 miles one way
Elevation gain: 450 feet, loss 100 feet
Allow 2 hours one way
Usually open June through September
High point: 9,350 feet
Topographic map:
    Map of adequate scale unavailable

During early July the slopes midway along the hike to Big Fish Lake support one of the most superb wild flower displays in northern Colorado and a stroll through this garden is a delightful and unforgettable experience. If you want to extend the trip you can continue another four miles, climbing 2,000 feet, to the plateau where trails go to Twin Lakes (No. 3) and Wall Lake (No. 4). The route of this side trek is easy to follow but the possible severe blowdown of dead trees during the first mile may cause the going to be very tedious.

Drive on Colorado 13-789 to the junction of Colorado 132 two miles northeast of Meeker. Turn southeast and after 30 miles leave the paved surface and begin traveling on a dirt road. Nine miles farther turn right where a sign points to Trappers Lake. Continue four miles to a sign on the south side of the road identifying the entrance to Himes Peak Campground. (U.S. Forest Service maps show it as Lynx Creek Campground.) Turn right and go downhill for 0.3 mile to a sign stating Big Fish Lake 3 and park in one of the few spaces here.

Drop slightly then curve right and walk across a grassy area. Descend to a bridge across the North Fork of the White River, climb briefly and several hundred feet from the span go through a metal gate. Traverse the grass and tree covered valley wall at a very moderate grade. At the north end of a huge meadow where an arrow points right keep left on the main trail and continue traversing gradually uphill through a marvelous flower garden. Yellow-green Indian paintbrush — the bracts of some tipped

with pink, little purple elephant heads and scarlet gilia add bright dots of color to the blue hues of the plentiful forget-me-nots and columbines. Tall chiming bells grow along the moister portions of the trail.

Beyond the large meadow come to a grassy, brushy area and cross several small streams. Drop slightly into a little depression then climb out of it and come to the north end of Big Fish Lake. Follow the trail along the east shore to observe a cluster of red columbine. Although columbine, a member of the buttercup family, grows over much of the northern hemisphere, the species vary from region to region and this red variety is not common in northern Colorado.

Except for the possible exasperating stretch of blowdown, the side trip to the plateau is an enjoyable extension of the hike. To make this climb, continue on the trail along the east side of the lake. Follow along the east edge of a large meadow in the woods. This is the only portion of the route that is faint. Continue through woods, veering slightly left, enter the area of blowdown and begin switchbacking up the slope. Come to a bench, cross it and switchback up the open face of a wall and after a short distance come to the edge of a swampy meadow. Follow the poles across it then resume climbing in woods. Come to the lush grass at the edge of the plateau and climb several hundred yards along a faint path to the junction with the trail that runs along the plateau. Turn right and hike 2.2 miles southwest to reach Twin Lakes or go left and travel 2.5 miles southeast to Wall Lake.

16

Meadow below Big Fish Lake

3 TWIN LAKES

One day trip or backpack
Distance: 6 miles one way
Elevation gain: 1,425 feet, loss 100 feet
Allow 3 to 3½ hours one way
Usually open mid-June through September
High point: 11,025 feet
Topographic map:
   U.S.G.S. Glenwood Springs, Colo.
   30′   **1927**

One-half of the hike to Twin Lakes is across the 11,000 foot high plateau south of Trappers Lake. As you wind up the steep slopes from the lake you can see no indication of what to expect at the crest and when you reach the rim you will be pleasantly surprised by the unique landscape: clusters of trees, low peaks and tarns are scattered over the grassy, rolling terrain that stretches for miles across the plateau. An interesting side trip can be made to Big Marvine Peak, west of Twin Lakes, one of the highest points in the area. You will have good views of this block of stone and grass during the final portion of the hike. Because of the open, gentle nature of the terrain, the number of other possible cross-country side trips is nearly infinite. A few well-defined trails also cross the plateau. A four mile path to Big Fish Lake (No. 2) leaves the main route at 3.7 miles and, although the descent is along an easily followed trail, one mile may be through severe blowdown. Carry water as the sources along the hike may not be dependable.

Proceed on Colorado 13-789 to the junction of Colorado 132 two miles northeast of Meeker. Turn southeast and after 30 miles leave the paved surface and begin traveling on a dirt road. Nine miles farther turn right where a sign points to Trappers Lake. Continue eight miles to a fork just beyond a lodge on a bluff up to your left. Turn right as indicated by a sign pointing to Trappers Lake Campground, and after 1¼ miles keep right at the entrances to the first two campgrounds and left at the entrance to the third. Drive an additional one-third mile and

where you pass a small parking area on your right continue on the main road to its end at a large turnaround. A sign stating Trappers Lake ¾ marks the trailhead.

Climb several yards to the crest of a little ridge then descend toward Trappers Lake. Stay on the west side of the small bay and walk through grass. Just before the trees resume along the shore come to an unsigned fork and keep right. Begin heading away from the lake, climbing moderately. At 1.0 mile, just south of Anderson Lake, come to a sign identifying the Trappers Lake Loop Trail. Keep straight and a few yards farther come to a sign listing mileages to Wall and Twin Lakes. Climb at a steady, moderate grade through sparse woods toward the basin along the wall. Cross a small stream and continue uphill in occasional switchbacks. As you gain elevation you will be able to look down onto Trappers Lake. Near the crest traverse up an open slope where snow remains until mid-July. Come to a pond and signs at the edge of the plateau, plus the junction of the trail to Wall Lake (No. 4).

Turn right and walk across the green, rolling terrain for 0.5 mile to the junction of the trail to Big Fish Lake. Keep straight (left) and climb slightly to a rim of trees. Descend gradually and continue across the open slopes with minor ups and downs past many tarns. Tall poles mark the easily followed route. Near 5.5 miles curve west and come above the southeast end of the larger of the Twin Lakes. Although campsites at the lakes are not good, many satisfactory spots can be found in the scattered clusters of trees nearby.

Twin Lakes and Big Marvine Peak

4 WALL LAKE

One day trip or backpack
Distance: 4.5 miles one way
Elevation gain: 1,500 feet
Allow 2½ to 3 hours one way
Usually open mid-June through September
High point: 11,000 feet
Topographic map:
    U.S.G.S. Glenwood Springs, Colo.
    30′   **1927**

The trail to Wall Lake climbs along the route to Twin Lakes for the first three miles to the edge of the plateau high above Trappers Lake then heads southeast for 1.5 miles across the grassy, rolling terrain. You can make a loop by continuing beyond Wall Lake across the plateau then winding down the wall and returning to Trappers Lake along the trail from Fraser Lake (No. 5). This circuit would add 2.5 miles and negligible elevation gain. Carry drinking water as the sources along the hike are not dependable.

Drive on Colorado 13-789 to the junction of Colorado 132 two miles northeast of Meeker. Turn southeast and after 30 miles leave the paved surface and begin traveling on a dirt road. Nine miles farther turn right where a sign points to Trappers Lake. Continue eight miles to a fork just beyond a lodge on a bluff up to your left. Turn right as indicated by a sign pointing to Trappers Lake Campground, and after 1¼ miles keep right at the entrances to the first two campgrounds and left at the entrance to the third. Drive an additional one-third mile and where you pass a small parking area on your right continue on the main road to its end at a large turnaround. A sign stating Trappers Lake ¾ marks the trailhead.

Climb several yards to the crest of a little ridge then descend toward Trappers Lake. Stay on the west side of the small bay and walk through grass. Just before the trees resume along the shore come to an unsigned fork and keep right. Begin heading away from the lake, climbing moderately. At 1.0 mile, just south of Anderson Lake, come to a sign identifying the Trappers Lake Loop Trail. Keep straight and a few yards farther come to a sign listing mileages to Wall and Twin Lakes.

Climb at a steady, moderate grade through sparse woods toward the basin beneath the wall. Cross a small stream and continue uphill in occasional switchbacks. As you gain elevation you will be able to look down onto Trappers Lake. Near the crest traverse up an open slope where snow tends to remain until mid-July and come to a tarn and signs at the edge of the plateau and the junction of the trail to Twin Lakes.

Keep left, pass several ponds and follow the multi-tracked trail across the grassy, rolling terrain. Stakes and several cairns mark the already obvious route. At 4.0 miles you will be able to see Wall Lake from the last of several slight rises. Curve left through a swampy area then come to the tree-rimmed lake. The best campsites are along the northwest shoreline.

20

Trappers Peak

Trappers Lake

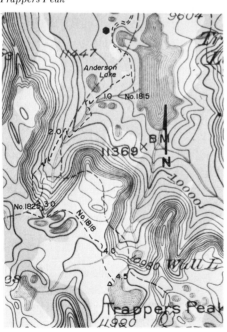

21

5 FRASER LAKE

One day trip or backpack
Distance: 5 miles one way
Elevation gain: 1,100 feet
Allow 2½ to 3 hours one way
Usually open June through September
High point: 10,650 feet
Topographic map:
   U.S.G.S. Glenwood Springs, Colo.
   30′   1927

The ghostly images of spruce trees killed by an infestation of bark beetles are reflected on the waters of Fraser Lake. However, most of this hike up the long valley south of Trappers Lake is through healthy woods and past large, lush meadows. You are urged to continue climbing on the main trail one mile beyond Fraser Lake to the rim of the immense plateau that extends south and west from the crest of the wall above the lake. If you want to go even farther you could follow the trail that heads south to Island Lake or make a loop trip by returning along the route to Wall Lake (No. 4). The standing dead spruce along the final mile of trail are susceptible to being blown down by strong winds so be alert while walking through this stretch and do not rest or camp under the affected trees.

Proceed on Colorado 13-789 to the junction of Colorado 132 two miles northeast of Meeker. Turn southeast and after 30 miles leave the paved surface and begin traveling on a dirt road. Nine miles farther turn right where a sign points to Trappers Lake. Continue eight miles to a fork, keep left and drive one-third mile to parking.

Traverse up the slope for about 100 yards to a level, open area above the northern tip of Trappers Lake where a sign lists mileages to Wall, Little Trappers and Fraser Lakes. (You can reach this junction from the several campgrounds near the northwestern end of Trappers Lake by following the path that drops from the southeast edge of the lowest camping area to the lake. Turn left, follow the path along the north shore, cross the outlet creek on a large bridge and climb several yards to the sign.)

Keep straight (left) at the sign and travel just above the northeast shore with a few slight ups and downs. Pass the dock and boat tender's cabin, keep left on the main trail where a side path goes downhill and at 0.5 mile traverse to the east above another cabin. Just beyond this second building come to the junction of the trail to Little Trappers Lake (No. 6). Keep right and after a short distance come to the crossing of the outlet from Little Trappers Lake. If the flow is heavy you may want to scramble up the bank for a better ford. Walk in woods at a generally level grade near the shore of Trappers Lake for one mile then veer away from the lake and begin climbing at a mostly steady, moderate grade. Near 2.0 miles drop to a large meadow and the junction of the very faint Trappers Lake Loop Trail. Keep straight (left) and walk around the east and south edges of the clearing then curve left into woods. The large cirque along the high, steep wall to the southwest is called The Amphitheatre. Enter a second, smaller meadow and climb through open woods to an easy ford at 2.5 miles. Walk beside a treeless, brushy area on the valley floor for 0.2 mile then recross the stream. Climb at an irregular, but never severe, grade along the grass and tree covered slope. Enter an area of dead spruce and continue uphill to a sign at 4.9 miles identifying the spur to Fraser Lake. Turn right and descend gradually for 0.1 mile to the shore. A good lunch stop is across the inlet.

To make the recommended climb to the rim, continue uphill from the junction at 4.9 miles. Switchback and keep climbing a short distance to a large grassy basin. Resume climbing in switchbacks to a lush little bench then come to a second one with tarns. During the climb you will be able to see Fraser Lake directly below and down the length of the valley to Trappers Lake. Wind up through a little rocky defile below the rim to the signs indicating the routes to Island Lake and Wall Lake.

Meadow above Trappers Lake

Trail junction above Fraser Lake

6 LITTLE TRAPPERS LAKE

One-half day trip
Distance: 1.5 miles one way
Elevation gain: 350 feet
Allow 1 hour one way
Usually open June through September
High point: 9,950 feet
Topographic map:
    U.S.G.S. Glenwood Springs, Colo.
    30′   **1927**

The short, easy trip to Little Trappers Lake is a good choice for a first hike in the Flat Tops before tackling the longer and more strenuous treks in the area. After following the northeast shore of Trappers Lake for one-half mile the trail turns east and passes just above the tip of Coffin Lake before paralleling the outlet creek to the northwest end of Little Trappers Lake. During early July wild flowers, including two varieties of Indian paintbrush, forget-me-nots, tall chiming bells and columbine, brighten the slopes beside the trail. The main route continues beyond Little Trappers Lake for six miles to Mosquito Lake and a short distance past the latter to Stillwater Reservoir.

Drive on Colorado 13-789 to the junction of Colorado 132 two miles northeast of Meeker. Turn southeast and after 30 miles leave the paved surface and begin traveling on a dirt road. Nine miles farther turn right where a sign points to Trappers Lake. Continue eight miles to a fork just beyond a lodge on a bluff up to your left. Keep left and drive beside the creek to the road's end at a large parking area one-third mile from the fork.

Traverse up the slope for about 100 yards to a level, open area above the northern tip of Trappers Lake where a sign lists mileages to Wall, Little Trappers and Fraser Lakes. (You can reach this junction from the several campgrounds near the northwestern end of Trappers Lake by following the path that drops from the southeast edge of the lowest camping area to the lake. Turn left, follow the path along the north shore, cross the outlet creek on a large bridge and climb several yards to the sign.) Many large cutthroat trout slowly swim under the bridge but before you will be able to discern their leisurely, graceful movements you will need to allow a few minutes for your eyes to adjust to the lack of contrast between the fish and the creek bottom. (Polarized sunglasses help.) Marmots are plentiful in the rocks and grass above the stream and, if you are lucky, you may see a duck and her chicks paddling near the shore.

Keep straight (left) at the sign and travel just above the northeast shore with a few slight ups and downs. Pass the dock and boat tender's cabin, keep left on the main trail where a side path goes downhill and at 0.5 mile traverse to the east above another cabin. Just beyond this second building come to the junction of the trail to Fraser Lake (No. 5).

Keep left and after several feet pass a sign indicating you are on the Stillwater Trail. Climb and drop slightly to a spot above the west end of Coffin Lake. Curve right, descend for several yards into a meadow and pass a register. Climb gradually then traverse above the outlet of Little Trappers Lake and walk on the level for a short distance before coming to the northwest end of the lake.

The Amphitheatre—Trappers Lake

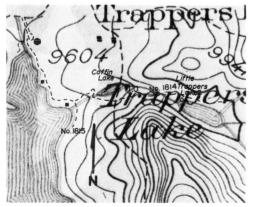

Little Trappers Lake

7

HAHNS PEAK

One day trip
Distance: 2 miles one way
Elevation gain: 1,470 feet
Allow 1½ to 2 hours one way
Usually open June through September
High point: 10,839 feet
Topographic map:
    U.S.G.S. Hahns Peak, Colo.
    7.5′   **1962**

Hahns Peak, situated 11 miles south of the Wyoming boarder in an area profusely sprinkled with the abandoned tunnels of small mines, is the most northerly of the hikes described in this guide. During the climb of the pyramid-shaped mountain you will be able to see over the lush valleys and timbered slopes of the Routt National Forest into Wyoming and from the summit you can look down onto Pearl and Steamboat Lakes. Carry drinking water as none is available along the climb.

One mile west of Steamboat Springs turn north from U.S. 40 onto Routt County Road 129 at the sign pointing to Hahns Peak and Clark. Proceed 18 miles to the community of Clark and 0.5 mile farther keep left at a fork. One mile beyond the junction the pavement ends then resumes again after three more miles but four miles farther stops permanently. Eleven miles from the fork come to the small settlement of Columbine and turn right onto the unmarked road just beyond the first building on your right. Follow the rough but not steep road for one mile to a point where it curves uphill to the left and a side road joins from the right. You can leave your car here or drive the final

distance. Curve left and walk or drive uphill for 0.5 mile to a fork where one branch continues straight for a few hundred feet before coming to private property and the other curves left. A sign at this junction indicates the route to Hahns Peak. If you have driven this far, leave your car here.

Curve left and walk along the jeep road, keeping right where it forks after a few hundred feet. Climb moderately for 0.2 mile then traverse a less densely wooded slope. Avalanche lilies and other wild flowers brighten the landscape during midsummer. Travel along a grassy, treeless slope and where you have your first view down onto the community of Columbine be watching for a sign on your right identifying the beginning of the trail proper. This sign may be on the ground and not obvious. Turn right and climb moderately for a few hundred feet then switchback to the left.

Continue up at a steady grade along the wooded northwestern slope then at 1.0 mile curve right. Switchback a few times then come to a sparsely wooded area near timberline. Wind up through the open area for several hundred feet then cross over to the south side of the ridge. Traverse along the lower shoulder of the mountain to a saddle at timberline where an old, wooden cabin adjoins the trail. Just above the structure cross a road and resume climbing on a now very rocky trail. Curve south and soon begin winding up at a steady, moderate grade near the crest of the summit ridge, passing an old mine shaft at the end of one switchback. The final few hundred feet to the wooden lookout on the summit is along the slightly broader and more gentle crest.

26

Hahns Peak

8 MICA BASIN

One day trip or backpack
Distance: 5 miles one way
Elevation gain: 2,050 feet
Allow 3 to 3½ hours one way
Usually open mid-June through September
High point: 10,450 feet
Topographic map:
    U.S.G.S. Mount Zirkel, Colo.
    7.5′   **1955**

The Mt. Zirkel Wilderness straddles the crest of the Park Range, the string of mountains that form the western boundary of North Park. Eight trails described in this guide penetrate the preserve. The trips to Mica Basin, Gilpin Lake (No. 9) and Gold Creek Lake (No. 10) begin on the west side at the abandoned mining community of Slavonia and the trailheads for the hikes to Three Island Lake (No. 11) and North Lake (No. 12) are only a few miles away by road. The remaining three treks, Seven Lakes (No. 17), Lake Katherine (No. 18) and Rainbow and Slide Lakes (No. 19), begin on the east side of the Park Range.

Mica Basin lies above the head of a long, narrow valley and is rimmed on three sides by high, rocky walls. Mica Lake occupies a portion of the basin floor. Early in the summer the variety and density of wild flowers growing along the trail offer one of the best displays seen in the Mt. Zirkel Wilderness.

Through June snow may cover portions of the final two miles but because of the nature of the terrain you should have no trouble finding Mica Lake. This last stretch also includes one ford and some marshy sections.

Drive on U.S. 40 one mile west of Steamboat Springs to the junction of the Elk River Road (Routt County 129) where a sign points to Hahns Peak and Clark. Turn north and proceed 18 miles to the settlement of Clark. One mile farther come to the junction of the road to the Seedhouse Guard

Station and turn right, leaving the paved surface. After five miles keep left at a fork and four miles farther keep left (straight) at the junction of the South Fork Elk River Road. Continue three miles to a sign pointing to Sheep Driveway and listing several mileages. A few hundred feet beyond the sign come to a large parking area.

Walk along the jeep road that begins at the north edge of the turnaround for 0.1 mile to an old cabin on your right. Just beyond the structure come to the junction of the trail to Gold Creek Lake and keep left as indicated by the sign identifying the Gilpin Trail. Where the path forks after 100 feet you can follow either one. Hike at a very moderate grade through an area of grass and scattered aspen and firs then travel above Gilpin Creek. Continue across sparsely-wooded slopes and cross a side creek that has been dammed by beavers a short distance upstream. Cross a few other small side streams and begin traveling along more rocky and wooded terrain. A few of the many varieties of wild flowers you will see during this first part of the hike include Indian paintbrush, columbine, shooting stars and larkspur. Farther along the trip these are replaced by avalanche lilies, buttercups and globe flowers. Pass the sign that marks the Wilderness boundary and at 1.5 miles come to the junction of the trail to Gilpin Lake.

Keep left and walk on the level through woods for 0.2 mile, switchback up more open slopes then traverse in woods above Mica Creek. The trail rises at a steeper grade then levels off before coming near a cascade. Turn left and wind up around rocks to a bench then walk on the level toward the creek. Go through a little defile to the southern edge of a basin and descend to a stream crossing. If you are hiking early in the summer you may want to cross on a log jam several hundred yards upstream. The remaining two miles of the hike climb to the north through open woods and grassy areas at an uneven grade along the eastern side of the valley not too far above the floor. At 4.7 miles begin rising more steeply and after 0.2 mile come to gentle slopes just south of Mica Lake. A trail goes west and north from the south edge of the basin, climbing over the shoulder of Little Agnes Mountain.

Mica Creek

Mica Lake in June

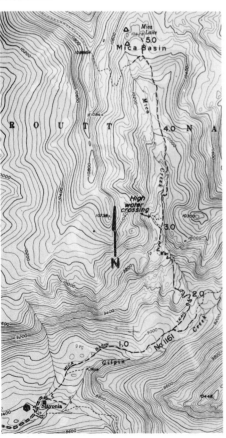

9 GILPIN LAKE

One day trip or backpack
Distance: 5 miles one way
Elevation gain: 1,950 feet
Allow 3 to 3½ hours one way
Usually open late June through September
High point: 10,350 feet
Topographic map:
    U.S.G.S. Mount Zirkel, Colo.
    7.5′   **1955**

The setting of Gilpin Lake is one of the most scenic in the Mt. Zirkel Wilderness. The lake rests on a bench and although bordered by peaks on three sides, the west edge is mostly open, creating the feeling of an aerie. For a good view of this scene you can follow the trail around the eastern shore to a little pass above the south end of the lake. After the end of June you can make an interesting but strenuous loop by continuing down from the pass through woods and meadows to Gold Creek Lake (No. 10). This highly recommended trip would add 2.5 miles and 400 feet of elevation gain. The one ford encountered on the circuit is deep until late summer.

Proceed on U.S. 40 one mile west of Steamboat Springs to the junction of the Elk River Road (Routt County 129) where a sign points to Hahns Peak and Clark. Turn north and drive 18 miles to the settlement of Clark. One mile farther come to the junction of the road to the Seedhouse Guard Station and turn right, leaving the paved surface. After five miles keep left at a fork and four miles farther keep left (straight) at the junction of the South Fork Elk River Road. Continue three miles to a sign pointing to Sheep Driveway and listing several mileages. Stay on the main road, and find parking a few hundred feet beyond the sign.

Walk along the jeep road that begins at the north edge of the turnaround for 0.1 mile to an old cabin on your right. Just beyond the structure come to the junction of the trail to Gold Creek Lake. If you make the recommended loop you will be returning along this route. Keep left as indicated

by the sign identifying the Gilpin Trail and listing several mileages and where the path forks after 100 feet you can follow either one as the branches join after a short distance. Hike at a very moderate grade through an area of grass and scattered aspen and firs then travel above Gilpin Creek. Continue across sparsely wooded slopes, cross a few small side streams and begin traveling along more rocky and wooded terrain. Pass the sign that marks the Wilderness boundary and come to the junction of the trail to Mica Basin (No. 8).

Keep straight (right) and travel on the level then climb slightly to the ford of Mica Creek. Although the crossing is not difficult, you probably will get wet feet. Continue moderately uphill, switchbacking a few times. Enter deeper woods and traverse above Gilpin Creek. Continue in woods, passing through a swampy area and hopping across a narrow, deep stream at one point, and at 2.6 miles begin traveling on a well-maintained trail along the northwest edge of an immense swath of avalanche debris. Climb moderately and just beyond the northern end of the rubble reach a crest above a basin. Come to the ford of Gilpin Creek and if you want a drier crossing, bushwhack 200 yards upstream to a log. Switchback up in woods and pass through a small clearing then continue uphill, curving gradually south, and come to the north end of Gilpin Lake.

To make the loop or just to reach the little pass, follow the path along the east shore of the lake and near its southeast end begin switchbacking then go through a rocky area to the crest. From the pass descend to a bench, walk along it then switchback down through woods. About one mile from the crest keep right at the unsigned junction of the trail to Red Dirt Pass and one-third mile farther at the edge of a meadow keep right again at the unsigned junction of the route to Ute Pass. Follow beside a creek for a short distance and come to a large stream. Go upstream several yards for a better ford. Walk on the level to a signed junction of the Wyoming Trail, continue in the same direction you had been traveling and climb a low rise. Several hundred yards farther come near the north shore of Gold Creek Lake.

Ice on Gilpin Lake

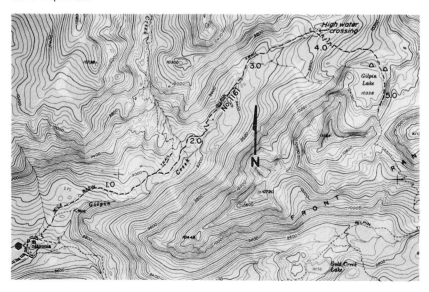

10 GOLD GREEK LAKE

One day trip or backpack
Distance: 3 miles one way
Elevation gain: 1,160 feet
Allow 2 hours one way
Usually open June through September
High point: 9,560 feet
Topographic map:
   U.S.G.S. Mount Zirkel, Colo.
   7.5′   1955

The narrow, steep-sided, wooded valley the trail traverses for the three miles to Gold Creek Lake is a complementary contrast to the gentle, open slopes of the large alpine valley that extends to the northeast from the lake. You probably will want to allow some extra time for exploring this latter area. Although most of the trail climbs gradually or moderately, the grade for 0.5 mile near the end of the hike is steep.

If you are backpacking, three long side trips are possible from Gold Creek Lake: trails to Red Dirt Pass and Ute Pass go four and three miles to the northeast, and the Wyoming Trail, which you followed during the three miles to the lake, continues far to the south. Refer to the last paragraph of Trail No. 9 (Gilpin Lake) for information about the first parts of these side trips. Also, you can do the hike to Gold Creek Lake as a scenic but strenuous loop by combining it with the trip to Gilpin Lake.

Drive on U.S. 40 one mile west of Steamboat Springs to the junction of the Elk River Road (Routt County 129) where a sign points to Hahns Peak and Clark. Turn north and proceed 18 miles to the settlement of Clark. One mile farther come to the junction of the road to the Seedhouse Guard Station and turn right, leaving the paved surface. After five miles keep left at a fork and four miles farther keep left (straight) at the junction of the South Fork Elk River Road that goes to the trailheads for the hikes to Three Island Lake (No. 11) and

North Lake (No. 12). Continue three miles to a sign pointing to Sheep Driveway and listing several mileages. Stay on the main road and a few hundred feet beyond the sign come to a large parking area.

Walk along the jeep road that begins at the north edge of the turnaround for 0.1 mile to an old cabin on your right identified by a sign stating Slavonia Mining District — August, 1905. Just beyond the structure come to the junction of the trail to Mica Basin (No. 8) and Gilpin Lake. Keep right, as indicated by the sign identifying the Gold Creek Trail and listing several mileages, and walk on the level through grass and aspen. Pass a large cabin off the trail on your right and cross a bridge over Gilpin Creek then enter a band of evergreens before continuing on the level through an attractive grove of aspen and grass. Begin climbing moderately and curve gradually right to an overlook high above Gold Creek. Hike along the wooded slope and eventually walk beside the creek. Traverse a grassy wall, enter an area of boulders, grass and trees where you may see and hear some marmots then climb along the wall through a second open stretch just before the crossing of Gilpin Creek on two small logs at 1.7 miles.

The trail on the opposite side is obvious at first but eventually becomes faint. However, blazes on the trees indicate the way so you should have no trouble staying on the correct route. Climb parallel to, but not always beside, Gold Creek then recross Gold Creek by an easy ford and after a short distance come to the junction of the signed side path to Gold Creek Falls. Keep straight (right) and climb through woods along the increasingly steep and rocky trail for one-half mile. Begin traveling at a gradual grade and after 0.1 mile come to the west end of Gold Creek Lake. To reach the open terrain along the valley floor continue along the trail for another 0.2 mile.

Columbine and Aspen

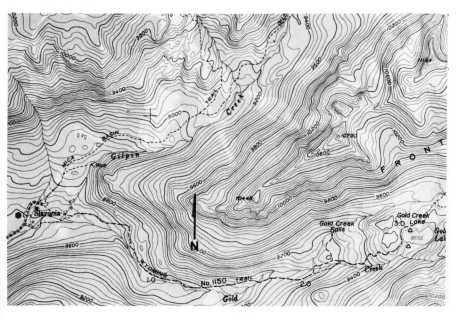

11 THREE ISLAND LAKE

One day trip or backpack
Distance: 3 miles one way
Elevation gain: 1,300 feet
Allow 2 hours one way
Usually open June through early October
High point: 9,880 feet
Topographic map:
  U.S.G.S. Mount Zirkel, Colo.
  7.5'   1955

Three Island Lake lies in a basin ringed on three sides by low, densely wooded slopes near the west central edge of the Mt. Zirkel Wildnerness. This hike and the one to Gold Creek Lake (No. 10) are the shortest of the five trips into the west side of the preserve. The moderate climb to the lake is an easy one day hike, but the many campsites along the shore make the trek a good choice for a short backpack. If you want to extend the hike and feel adventuresome, you could attempt to follow the trail that climbs over the wooded slope to the east of the lake then heads south past Beaver Lake to the Continental Divide and the Wyoming Trail. However, this route probably is not clear of snow until early July.

Proceed on U.S. 40 one mile west of Steamboat Springs to the junction of the Elk River Road (Routt County 129) where a sign points to Hahns Peak and Clark. Turn north and drive 18 miles to the settlement of Clark. One mile farther come to the junction of the road to the Seedhouse Guard Station and turn right, leaving the paved surface. After five miles keep left at a fork and four miles farther come to the junction of the South Fork Elk River Road. Turn right as indicated by the sign listing mileages to the Three Island Lake Trail and North Lake Trail (No. 12) and after a short distance cross the Middle Fork of the Elk River on a bridge. One mile from the junction curve up to the left on the main road where a spur goes right to Box Canyon Viewpoint and one mile farther come to a sign on your right pointing across the road

to the beginning of the Three Island Lake Trail and listing several mileages. Parking is available west of the sign.

Cross the road, as indicated by the arrows, to the trail that climbs along the bank in an easterly direction. After several yards switchback a few times then walk through a vale of aspen and grass. Switchback once more and come to the junction of the trail to Seedhouse Guard Station. Turn right and traverse the wooded slope at a gradual grade. Pass through a band of evergreens and after crossing two small side streams you will have views through aspen boughs down into the valley formed by the South Fork of the Elk River. At 1.4 miles come to a knob of boulders and curve east into the side valley that holds Three Island Creek. Walk at a very moderate grade for 0.1 mile then climb and drop slightly.

For the next 0.7 mile the route climbs through woods with occasional short switchbacks and the trail alternates between traveling close to Three Island Creek and a short distance from it. The route crosses several small side streams and bright wild flowers are scattered beside the trail. Near 2.4 miles begin hiking at a more moderate then level grade and come to the southwest edge of a large meadow. In addition to the many campsites at the lake, a few good spots are available in this clearing near the wide, deep outlet creek. Walk along the south edge of the meadow then reenter woods and after a few hundrd feet come to the north end of Three Island Lake. The best campsites are along the north shoreline.

34

Three Island Lake

12 NORTH LAKE

One day trip or backpack
Distance: 4.5 miles one way
Elevation gain: 1,800 feet
Allow 2½ to 3 hours one way
Usually open mid-June through September
High point: 10,300 feet
Topographic map:
    U.S.G.S. Mount Ethel, Colo.
    7.5′   1955

The relatively short but strenuous climb to shallow North Lake, the most southerly destination of the five hikes on the west side of the Mt. Zirkel Wilderness described in this guide, travels through dense forest for almost the entire distance. A trail continues east from the lake to the Continental Divide and the junction with the Wyoming Trail that runs north and south along many miles of the crest.

Drive on U.S. 40 one mile west of Steamboat Springs to the junction of the Elk River Road (Routt County 129) where a sign points to Hahns Peak and Clark. Turn north and proceed 18 miles to the settlement of Clark. One mile farther come to the junction of the road to Seedhouse Guard Station and turn right, leaving the paved surface. After five miles keep left at a fork and four miles farther come to the junction of the South Fork Elk River Road. The road that continues straight goes to the trailheads for the hikes to Mica Basin (No. 8), Gilpin Lake (No. 9) and Gold Creek Lake (No. 10). Turn right as indicated by the sign listing mileages to the Three Island Lake Trail and the North Lake Trail and after a short distance cross the Middle Fork of the Elk River on a bridge. One mile from the junction curve up to the left on the main road where a spur goes right to Box Canyon Viewpoint. One mile farther pass a sign on your right marking the beginning of the Three Island Lake Trail (No. 11) and con-

tinue 1.5 miles to the end of the road where several parking spaces are available. The unmarked trail begins at the south edge of the turnaround.

Walk on the level through woods for a short distance and cross a wide stream. If logs have not been placed across the flow, early in the season you will get your feet wet. A few yards beyond the creek ford a smaller stream and several yards farther come to the junction of the unimproved trail to Dome Lake. Keep left and soon begin climbing in short switchbacks. Make a long traverse then resume winding up. Come to a level bench then climb at a steeper grade than that on the switchbacks. Eventually, the trail rises more gradually near the top of a broad slope then it travels along the crest for about two miles in dense woods.

Near 4.0 miles come to a small marshy meadow and on its far (southeast) side hop across a creek. Switchback up beside another stream just to the south of the one you jumped. After gaining about 200 feet of elevation cross this second creek and climb parallel to its south side for 0.2 mile to a small meadow where signs mark the Mt. Zirkel Wilderness boundary and point west to Wolverine Basin. Resume walking through woods, still paralleling the second stream, and 0.2 mile from the clearing turn right and come to the wide grassy shoreline on the north side of North Lake. A low, rocky hill rises to the southwest.

Stream crossing near the trailhead

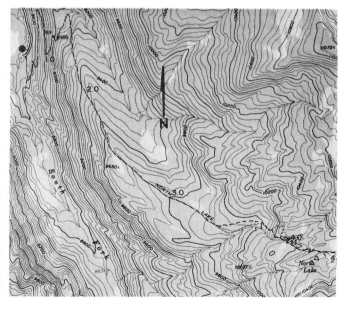

13 LONG LAKE (Routt County)

One day trip or backpack
Distance: 6 miles one way
Elevation gain: 2,200 feet, loss 150 feet
Allow 3 to 3½ hours one way
Usually open mid-June through September
High point: 9,850 feet
Topographic map:
   U.S.G.S. Storm Mountain, Colo.
   7.5'   1956
   (Last half of hike)

The two hikes that begin from Steamboat Springs and climb to the east are very different in character: During the short, but strenuous, ascent of Storm Peak (No. 14), already a developed ski area and still expanding, you are reminded constantly of the work of man on the landscape but on the hike to Long Lake you are in a wilderness setting from the beginning. The trail climbs through woods for the first two miles then traverses a rocky, rugged canyon wall before entering a gentle, lush valley. Wild flowers are profuse along portions of the hike during mid-summer but if you want to see 200 foot high Fish Creek Falls near the beginning of the hike at its best you will have to make the trip early in the season when the stream flow is the greatest. The grade is never steep and near the end of the trip it becomes very gradual.

Proceed on U.S. 40 to the south end of Steamboat Springs and just south of the municipal swimming pool turn east onto Routt County Road 32 where a sign points to National Forest Access and Fish Creek Falls. After a short distance begin traveling on a dirt surface and continue to a turna-round three miles from the highway. A sign stating Fish Creek Falls, high on a tree at the south edge of the loop, marks the beginning of the trail.

Descend on the path for 30 yards to a sign listing several mileages and turn left. Traverse downhill along the fenced trail to a large bridge over Fish Creek and a view of Fish Creek Falls. At the opposite end of the span the trail turns right and begins climbing. Switchback a few times and continue rising in woods and a few open areas. Wild flowers that brighten the forest floor along this section include paintbrush, aster, monkshood and fireweed. Near 1.6 miles come to a steep, treeless and rocky portion of the valley wall where you will have a good view of the rugged canyon formed by Fish Creek and the terrain the hike covers for the next several miles. Traverse slightly downhill and recross Fish Creek on a bridge.

Climb in a set of switchbacks then continue uphill along the slope, traversing a rock wall during one stretch. Switchback a few more times, come to the side path to Upper Fish Creek Falls and continue climbing by traversing and switchbacking. At the head of the canyon begin hiking along the gentle slopes of a broad, lush valley. Come to a meadow and travel near its northern edge. Continue at a very moderate grade along the slopes of grass, many wild flowers and scattered trees. You probably will hear and see marmots along this portion of the trek. Cross a small side stream and climb gradually for one-third mile to the northwest end of Long Lake. The main trail continues on the old, grass-covered dike that runs along the north shore of the lake then goes east and south to Lost Lake (No. 15) and other lakes.

Upper Fish Creek Falls

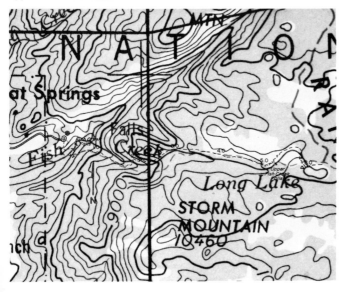

14 STORM PEAK

One day trip
Distance: 3 miles one way
Elevation gain: 3,500 feet
Allow 3½ to 4 hours one way
Usually open late May through September
High point: 10,460 feet
Topographic map:
Map of adequate scale unavailable

Storm Peak, rising to the southeast above the town of Steamboat Springs, is honey-combed with a network of ski runs and lifts and the steep, strenuous climb to the top of this mountain follows several of these routes. The first part of the ascent is along slopes of grass and wild flowers and during the entire trip you will have broad ranging views to the south and west.

If you want a shorter trip you can stop midway along the climb at the restaurant at the upper terminal of the gondola. To make the trip even easier, you could ride the gondola one or both ways. Inquire at the lower terminal for information about the current schedule and rates. Carry water as none is available along the hike if the gondola is not operating.

Drive on U.S. 40 to a sign pointing east to Steamboat Year Around Resort two miles south of the center of Steamboat Springs. Turn east and proceed 1.5 miles, keeping straight at all forks and passing many condominiums and shops in Steamboat Village, to a small parking area near the end of the road.

Walk along the lower road to the end of the Christy Chairlift and begin climbing steeply through the meadow, paralleling the cables. After 0.5 mile veer slightly left from the route of the lift and hike up a broad, treeless swath that is the See Me Run during the ski season. As you gain elevation you will have increasingly extensive views of the Yampa River Valley, the resort area and eventually the town of Steamboat Springs. Come to a crest where a few large boulders rest amidst the grass and several varieties of wild flowers, continue climbing and cross a dirt road. Keep climbing to a wide, smooth road covered with grass stubble, the Sitz Run, and follow it for 300 yards to a flat, open area below the gondola. The remaining distance to the terminal follows the Heavenly Daze Run beneath the gondola. To locate the stairs to the balcony go to the southeast corner of the terminal. Included in the far-ranging views are the Flat Tops along the southwestern horizon.

To reach Storm Peak, head southeast from the building to the upper end of the Burgess Creek Lift at 2.0 miles. Traverse to the northeast below the crest of the ridge then cross a wide swath at an uphill angle and continue climbing along Rainbow Run to the edge of the trees near the meeting place of the upper end of the 4 Points Lift and the beginning of the Storm Peak Lift. Climb the final one-half mile to the summit. The higher mountain to the northeast originally was called Storm Mountain but was renamed to honor Buddy Werner, a native of Steamboat Springs who, during the late 1950's, was one of the world's best ski racers. He was killed in an avalanche while skiing in Switzerland.

Steamboat Springs from the gondola terminal

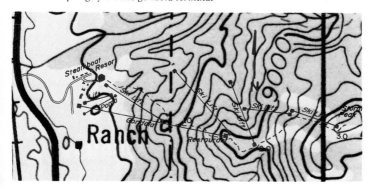

15 LOST LAKE

One-half day trip or backpack
Distance: 2 miles one way
Elevation gain: 100 feet, loss 260 feet
Allow 1 hour one way
Usually open July through September
High point: 10,020 feet
Topographic map:
   U.S.G.S. Storm Mountain, Colo.
   7.5'   1956

Two short, delightful hikes begin from the gentle, grassy slopes near Rabbit Ears Pass. The climb to the twin pinnacles of Rabbit Ears Peak (No. 16) travels through lush meadows for most of the ascent, but the trail to Lost Lake, located just west of the Continental Divide, passes through a more varied terrain of woods, meadows and lakes. If you want a longer trip you can continue beyond Lost Lake one mile on an almost level trail to Lake Elmo. From there the main route continues north for three-quarters mile to a junction where branches go east to Round Lake and Lake Perry and west to Long Lake (No. 13).

Proceed on U.S. 40 five miles northwest of the junction with Colorado 14 at Muddy Pass or 20 miles south and east of Steamboat Springs to a sign on the north side of the highway pointing to Dumont Lake. Turn north and drive about one-half mile to the junction with the old highway. Turn right and go one mile to the monument on your left marking Old Rabbit Ears Pass and a sign identifying Rabbit Ears Road and giving the mileage to the Divide Trail. Turn left onto the dirt road and after a few hundred yards come to a junction. Keep straight (left) and continue four miles through scenic terrain to a point where the road stops traversing steep slopes and enters a high, open almost level plateau. Continue one-half mile on the main road and at the north edge of a counter-clockwise curve come to a small picnic area on your right in woods marked by a sign stating Divide Trail and listing several mileages. Park beneath the trees.

Descend a steep old road bed through woods for 0.5 mile. In an open area where the road is blocked by large stones veer right onto a trail and, after traveling a few hundred yards through woods, come to the edge of a grassy valley. Walk through the meadow for a short distance then make an easy ford of Fishhook Creek. Enter a band of woods, pass through a small clearing then resume climbing in woods beside the lush valley.

Drop slightly and recross Fishhook Creek at the southern tip of Fishhook Lake. Walk along the southeastern shore, passing good campsites in the woods, and about three-quarters of the way along the length of the lake be watching for a tall wooden pole on the gentle, grassy slope above to your right. The route is faint for the next several hundred yards. Hike toward the pole and continue in a northeasterly direction across the clearing to a sign indicating the way to Lost Lake and Lake Elmo. Turn very slightly northwest (the Fishhook Lake side of the sign) and walk toward the woods where the well-defined trail resumes. Walk about 150 yards to the junction of the trail to Lake Elmo. Turn right and follow the short spur for 0.1 mile to the southern end of Lost Lake.

Fishhook Lake

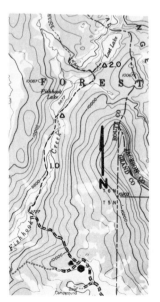

16 RABBIT EARS PEAK

One-half day trip
Distance: 3 miles one way
Elevation gain: 1,050 feet
Allow 1½ to 2 hours one way
Usually open June through September
High point: 10,654 feet
Topographic map:
   U.S.G.S. Rabbit Ears Peak, Colo.
   7.5'   1956

The 100 foot high twin summit pinnacles of Rabbit Ears Peak are one of northern Colorado's most distinctive landmarks. They can be identified as far north as Walden in North Park and almost as far south as Kremmling. The route to the peak, which follows an old jeep road, passes through lush rolling meadows, decorated with a profusion of wild flowers through mid-summer and scattered clusters of tall firs. Since the terrain is mostly open and gentle, you can make cross-country side trips to almost any destination you feel might be interesting. Carry drinking water as the sources along the trip may not be dependable.

Drive on U.S. 40 five miles northwest of the junction with Colorado 14 at Muddy Pass or 20 miles south and east of Steamboat Springs to a sign on the north side of the highway pointing to Dumont Lake. Turn north and drive about one-half mile to the junction with the old highway. Turn right and go one mile to the monument on your left marking Old Rabbit Ears Pass and a sign identifying Rabbit Ears Road. Turn left and park your car in the open space off the old highway.

Walk along Rabbit Ears Road for a few hundred yards to a junction and turn right. Continue at a moderate grade on an old jeep road, mostly through meadows. At 2.2 miles where you come to a sign stating Road Closed curve right and after a few hundred feet resume traveling on an obvious double track. Hike at a level grade through a grassy, tree-rimmed swale then curve left and climb very steeply for several hundred yards. The grade moderates and the route ends in woods just before the base of the western pinnacle. A 20 foot ladder simplifies the first pitch for those climbing the rock.

44

Ladder up the Western Ear

Rabbit Ears Peak from the west

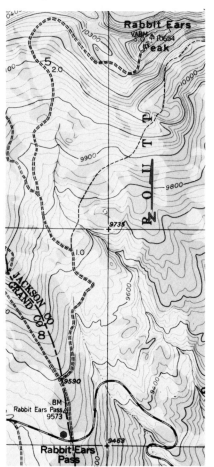

17 SEVEN LAKES

One day trip or backpack
Distance: 6 miles one way
Elevation gain: 1,740 feet
Allow 3½ to 4 hours one way
Usually open late June through September
High point: 10,740 feet
Topographic maps:
  U.S.G.S. Davis Peak, Colo.
  7.5'   1955
  U.S.G.S. Pearl, Colo.
  7.5'   1955

Seven Lakes and many neighboring tarns lie at the eastern edge of a high, immense plateau near the northern boundary of the Mt. Zirkel Wilderness. The gentle, mostly open nature of the terrain affords almost unlimited opportunity for easy cross-country exploration. This hike is one of the three trips that penetrate the east side of the Wilderness from North Park. Others are a short trip to Lake Katherine (No. 18) near the center of the preserve and a more demanding trek that climbs to Rainbow and Slide Lakes (No. 19).

Proceed on Colorado 125 nine miles north of Walden to the community of Cowdrey and turn west onto Jackson County Road 6 at the sign indicating the route to Lake John and Big Creek Lakes. The surface is paved for the first five miles. Eight miles from Cowdrey keep straight on the main road and 10 miles farther, just before the settlement of Pearl, turn left at the sign marking the road to Big Creek Lakes and Twisty Park. Although single track, the road, FS 2005, is level and has a good surface. Pass Big Creek Outpost after two miles and three miles farther turn left where a sign points to Big Creek Lake ½. Keep right at the fork just before the shore and drive above the lake, staying on the main road, to the end of the camping area where signs about 100 feet downslope mark the beginning of the Seven Lakes Trail. The signs are easy to miss until you are past the turnoff — if you curve sharply right and climb you have gone too far. Parkinig spaces for many cars are available at the signs.

Walk at an almost level grade through woods, periodically glimpsing the huge meadow along the southwest shore of lower Big Creek Lake. After a few minor ups and downs cross several small side streams on bridges then resume traveling on the level through an area that is a quagmire early in the season. Keep right where an unmarked path leads off to the left and after hiking above a small pond come to the signed junction of the side path to Upper Big Creek Lake. Keep right and climb moderately then traverse an open slope where you will have a good view down onto the lake. Contour along the slope of aspen and evergreens for a few hundred yards and cross a stream. Continue on the level, travel through deeper woods and at 2.1 miles after a slight climb enter the Mt. Zirkel Wilderness. A few yards beyond the boundary pass the short side path that drops to Big Creek Falls.

Keep right and traverse along the wooded slope above Big Creek and a brushy clearing. Begin climbing more noticeably, turn sharply north and after a few hundred yards cross a creek on a pole bridge at the southeast end of a little meadow. This is a good choice for a snack stop. A short distance beyond the span begin climbing in switchbacks. Come to a viewpoint where you can see a portion of North Park and Upper Big Creek Lake. Continue winding up to the crest at 4.2 miles, drop slightly, then begin a series of minor descents, rises and level stretches through attractive woods. Pass along the northern edge of a large, wild flower-covered meadow and beyond its end at 5.4 miles come to the junction of the trail to Davis Peak. Turn left and climb moderately through woods and small meadows for one-third mile to the junction of the connecting path to the trail to Davis Peak. Turn left again and traverse the grassy slope above a little valley. Since the trail becomes faint here, note landmarks for the next several hundred yards to facilitate your return. Curve right across the head of the valley and cross a little stream then turn left and come to the northern end of the Seven Lakes complex. Continue south and southeast to visit the remaining tarns. The Continental Divide runs along the crest of the ridge to the south.

Big Creek Falls

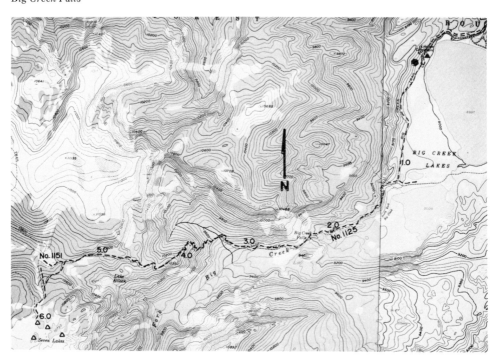

18 LAKE KATHERINE

One day trip
Distance: 2.5 miles one way
Elevation gain: 760 feet
Allow 1½ hours one way
Usually open mid-June through early October
High point: 9,870 feet
Topographic maps:
    U.S.G.S. Boettcher Lake, Colo.
    7.5'   1956
    U.S.G.S. Mount Ethel, Colo.
    7.5'   1955
    U.S.G.S. Pitchpine Mountain, Colo.
    7.5'   1955

The dam at Lake Katherine

The last mile of the hike to Lake Katherine, situated in the approximate geographic center of the Mt. Zirkel Wilderness, climbs beside the outlet creek and when you reach the stone and mortar dam across the narrow northeastern finger of the lake you will understand the reason for the debris you saw along the severely eroded banks of the stream. A sudden, powerful flow of water pushed a gaping hole through the base of the dam, rushed down the creek, gnawed at the banks, uprooted trees and dislodged boulders.

Although the trail is faint for a short distance near 1.3 miles and climbs moderately steeply for the last 0.5 mile, most of this short hike through woods and grassy clearings is gradual and easily followed.

Drive on Colorado 14 or 125 to the junction of Jackson County Road 12, located one mile south and west of Walden and marked by a sign pointing to Delaney Butte Lakes and Lake John. Turn west and after five miles curve right, staying on Jackson County 12, then three miles farther keep left on Jackson 12. The pavement soon ends and two miles from the previous fork curve right at the junction of the road that goes left to Delaney Butte Lakes. Proceed two miles then turn left onto Jackson County 16. After two miles the road becomes single lane and passes the buildings of the Lone Pine Ranch. Although narrow and sometimes rocky, the road is not steep for the remaining distance. One mile from the ranch keep right where a side road goes left, two miles farther enter Routt National Forest and

three miles from the forest boundary come to the end of the road. A sign stating Trail No. 1129 marks the beginning of the hike.

Climb gently through evergreen woods and across small grassy clearings, following a faint old double-track road for a short distance. Cross several small side streams and eventually enter deeper woods. At 1.2 miles come to the edge of a clearing littered with avalanche debris. Follow the trail for 150 feet into a rim of trees and after a few yards where the trail forks keep right. Drop slightly, cross a dilapidated pole bridge and continue down through a marshy meadow, traveling in the same direction you were headed as you crossed the bridge. After a few hundred feet be watching on your right for a pole with a sign on it stating Trail No. 1129. Continue through the meadow parallel, but not close, to the stream, watching for another pole about 50 yards from the first. From this second marker locate the third then at the latter look for a blaze on a tree that marks the resumption of the obvious route. Walk about 250 yards through woods to the crossing of Lone Pine Creek just above the confluence of the outlet stream from Lake Katherine. Go several yards upstream for a possible log crossing. On the opposite bank the trail makes a short switchback after a few yards then climbs moderately beside the outlet creek from Lake Katherine. Begin winding up at a steeper grade and after 0.5 mile come to the end of the lake. A shelter cabin and campsites are located in the woods near the southeast end of the dam.

Lake Katherine

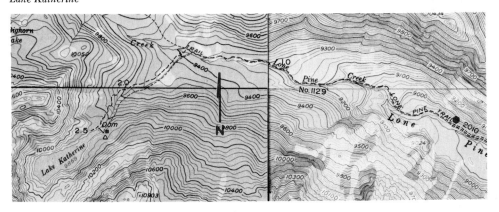

19 RAINBOW and SLIDE LAKES

One day trip or backpack
Distance: 6 miles one way
Elevation gain: 1,770 feet
Allow 3½ to 4 hours one way
Usually open late June through September
High point: 10,530 feet
Topographic maps:
    U.S.G.S. Mount Ethel, Colo.
    7.5′   **1955**
    U.S.G.S. Pitchpine Mountain, Colo.
    7.5′   **1955**

Slide Lake is the most southerly of the trips in the Mt. Zirkel Wilderness and a good choice for those who enjoy a moderately strenuous hike. The final 0.5 mile is cross-country and an interesting extension of the trek would be to continue on the faint main trail across the mountains to the north to Roxy Ann Lake. This side trip would add a total of six miles and 1,750 feet of elevation gain. The last mile of road to the trailhead is the roughest you will have to drive to reach any of the hikes described in this guide. Although passable in dry weather to all vehicles with moderate ground clearance, the stretch is narrow, steep and rocky.

Proceed on Colorado 14 or 125 to the junction of Jackson County Road 12, located one mile south and west of Walden and marked by a sign pointing to Delaney Butte Lakes and Lake John. Turn west and after five miles keep left on Jackson County 18. After another five miles turn left and soon begin traveling on an unpaved surface. Two miles from the previous junction keep straight on Jackson County 22, leaving Jackson County 5, and after four miles bear right at a fork. Continue the final three miles along an increasingly rough road to its end where many parking spaces are available beneath the trees. A sign at the west edge of the turnaround lists mileages to Rainbow, Slide and Roxy Ann Lakes.

Walk along the wide trail for 100 yards to a fork and keep left. Climb moderately on the rocky path through woods of small aspen and pines. At 0.8 mile come to the junction of the Grizzly Creek Trail and keep straight. After a short distance hike along the crest of a narrow ridge covered with aspen and brush then traverse along the southern slope where you can look southeast over a portion of North Park. At 0.4 mile from the junction abruptly come to a

flat area on the crest then begin traveling on the north side of the slope 700 feet above lush Livingston Park. At 2.1 miles the trail drops gradually then begins traveling through a level area that contains many short quagmires early in the season. Ford a stream at 2.5 miles and continue on the level then begin climbing. Descend slightly and travel above Middle Rainbow Lake before coming to the southeast end of Rainbow Lake.

The main trail traverses above the wooded southern shore of Rainbow Lake to the Wilderness boundary near the southwestern end where a sign points to Roxy Ann and Slide Lakes. Turn left and climb in a southwesterly direction then curve back toward the lake. Ford one creek, then a short distance farther, cross a second stream and several yards past the latter come to the third and largest creek. If you are hiking early in the season and the flow is heavy, turn left and climb steeply cross-country near the stream for about 150 yards. Where the grade moderates continue paralleling the creek and begin looking for a small log jam. Cross here and intersect the main trail that wound up near the north bank of the stream.

Hike uphill and go through some open, grassy areas where early in the summer globeflowers, avalanche lilies and other wild flowers thrive. Follow the trail for a few hundred feet as it curves left and crosses a grassy slope, heading toward the creek, then turn right and begin climbing cross-country. Continue uphill for one-third mile to an overlook above Slide Lake. Descend for 0.1 mile, losing 50 feet of elevation, to reach the shore.

To visit Roxy Ann Lake continue on the main trail and after a short distance curve west then north around the base of the rock and grass slope below Slide Lake.

Rainbow Lake

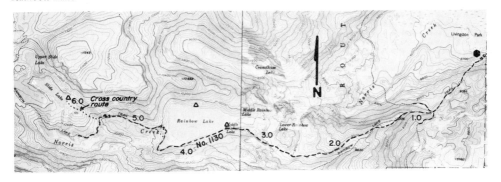

20 HYANNIS PEAK

One day trip or backpack
Distance: 5.5 miles one way
Elevation gain: 2,200 feet, loss 200 feet
Allow 3½ to 4 hours one way
Usually open June through September
High point: 11,602 feet
Topographic maps:
    U.S.G.S. Buffalo Peak, Colo.
    7.5′   **1956**
    U.S.G.S. Hyannis Peak, Colo.
    7.5′   **1956**

Usually, the summit of a mountain is a spot to just sit and look at the view. But the grassy area surrounding the twin rock outcroppings that comprise the top of Hyannis Peak invite exploration. The mountain is in the remote central portion of the Rabbit Ears Range that forms the southern boundary of North Park. From the summit you will be able to see Mount Zirkel to the northwest, North Park below to the north, the Medicine Bow Range to the northeast, Parkview Mountain to the east and, beyond it, a portion of the western side of Rocky Mountain National Park. The level crest of the Flat Tops are on the horizon to the southwest and the view extends south to the Holy Cross region.

Between 1.9 and 3.5 miles you will ford the Middle Fork of Arapaho Creek four times. Although the crossings are not difficult or dangerous, the flow is deep enough early in the season to cause wet feet. The final 0.6 mile is easy cross-country up an open slope of grass and scattered wild flowers.

Drive on Colorado 14 for 15.5 miles north of its junction with U.S. 40 at Muddy Pass or 17.5 miles south of its intersection with Colorado 125 just south of Walden to an unpaved side road heading southeast to the community of Rand and identified as Jackson County 28. Proceed on the dirt road for one mile to a fork and curve right onto Jackson County 11. Three miles farther keep left where the road branches and one mile beyond keep left at the sign pointing

to Bundy Park and Arapaho Lakes. After another three miles pass a Routt National Forest boundary sign; five miles farther keep left where a side road goes to Bundy Park. After another 1¼ miles, just beyond a sign identifying the East Fork of Arapaho Creek, look left for a faint side road that climbs back to the southeast above the large marshy area formed by the Middle Fork of Arapaho Creek. A few parking spaces are available along the shoulder.

Climb along the old road bed for a short distance then drop slightly and eventually begin hiking on a trail. Travel at a moderate grade through woods and pass a spring just below the trail then come to the edge of a small clearing. Curve right and walk near the edge of the open area then resume hiking through woods with a few slight drops. At 1.1 miles pass above a pond in a little depression and after a short, steep climb come to a semi-open slope above the Middle Fork of Arapaho Creek. Contour above the stream and at 1.5 miles enter a long meadow. Follow the tall poles across the grassy slope and cross a small stream at a campsite in some scattered evergreens.

Continue in the same direction and just before the south end of a smaller grassy area come to the first ford. Curve left on the opposite shore and shortly resume traveling on an obvious trail. After 0.2 mile recross the flow. Traverse the slope at a very moderate grade. As you proceed up the valley you'll note the trees become more sparse. At 2.7 miles pass a sign pointing to Carter Creek and continue along the slope. The route is faint on this stretch but it is not difficult to follow. Come to the third crossing at 3.5 miles and, after walking a few hundred yards along the south side, ford the stream once again. Continue traversing the slope and 0.4 mile from the crossing begin climbing more noticeably then curve left (north) into a broad side valley. Traverse the slope for three-quarters mile through an old burn. Cross a small creek and where the trail begins dropping to a larger stream turn left and begin the 0.6 mile cross-country climb to the two pinnacles on the crest. The main trail continues in a generally easterly direction across the open slopes for four miles to Sheep Mountain.

Looking southeast from Hyannis Peak

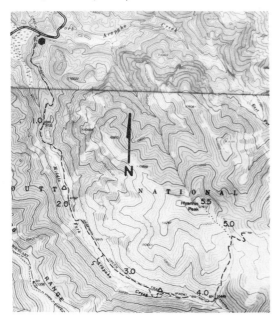

21 PARKVIEW MOUNTAIN

One day trip
Distance: 5.2 miles one way
Elevation gain: 3,495 feet
Allow 3½ to 5 hours one way
Usually open June through September
High point: 12,296 feet
Topographic maps:
   U.S.G.S. Parkview, Mtn., Colo.
   7.5'   1956
   U.S.G.S. Radial Mountain, Colo.
   7.5'   1956

From the summit of Parkview Mountain you can enjoy one of the most far-ranging panoramas in northern Colorado. Although the name of the massive peak probably applies to its location high above the southern end of North Park, you also will have views into Rocky Mountain National Park close to the east with an especially good sighting of the portion of Longs Peak between the Keyhole and the summit. The Park Range on the horizon to the northwest includes the Mt. Zirkel Wilderness and the Medicine Bow Range with the Rawah Wilderness in its center is on the skyline to the northeast. Below this latter chain is the Never Summer Range, the western boundary of Rocky Mountain National Park. The view extends south to the Holy Cross region and southwest to the area around Aspen and the distinctive level crest of the Flat Tops.

The first 3.8 miles of the hike climbs in woods along a rough jeep road to timberline then the route begins winding cross-country up slopes of grass and wild flowers to the broad, gentle summit ridge. Carry drinking water as sources along the hike may not be dependable.

Proceed on Colorado 125 five miles south of Willow Creek Pass or 16 miles north of the junction with U.S. 40 to a sign stating Parkview Mountain Trail at a rough road on the west side of the highway. This spot is 0.1 mile south of a road heading east and

downhill to the Vagabond Ranch, Still Water Pass and the Lost Lake Trail. A few parking spaces are available on the highway shoulder near the trailhead or a short distance down the Vagabond Ranch road.

Climb along the road for a short distance then curve left and walk above an old cabin. At 0.2 mile begin traveling to the west beside the edge of a small valley filled with brush and beaver ponds. Near its western end veer away from the swale and resume climbing in woods. The grade generally is moderate but periodically the road climbs at a somewhat steeper angle. At 1.8 miles come to a fork and turn right as indicated by the sign pointing to Parkview Mountain. Red metal tags imbedded in trees identify the correct route at several junctions farther along the road. Pass the remains of a pole pen and at 2.3 miles keep left at a fork. Two-tenths mile farther stay right and after another 0.2 mile keep left. The grade soon becomes very moderate as the route traverses to the north. Walk on the level for about one-quarter mile then watch for red tabs that mark a side road going left. This junction is across from a post on the right side of the main road.

Turn left and follow this side road through more scenic woods. Walk beside a small creek then just beyond a large clearing come to timberline at 3.8 miles. Continue on the road, rising moderately along a slope brightened in mid-summer with the rich yellow color of buttercups. As the grade steepens the track becomes faint and soon stops entirely. Look back and note landmarks so on the return you will be able to locate the spot where the road reenters the woods. Begin climbing cross-country toward the crest and as you gain elevation the waxy buttercup blossoms are replaced by tiny alpine forget-me-nots, the variety of Indian paintbrush with leaves of a yellow-green hue, gentians and other pert wild flowers. Seven-tenths mile from timberline come to the crest and hike along the ridge top at a very moderate grade. Do not walk along the snow just below the crest on the east side as it may be corniced. Soon you will be able to see the lookout house ahead to the northwest. Follow the path that traverses the western slope just below the crest for 0.2 mile to the summit.

Rabbit Ears Range from Parkview Mountain

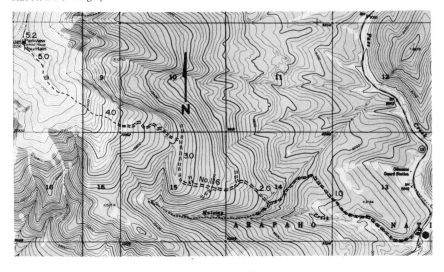

22 EAGLESMERE LAKES

One day trip or backpack
Distance: 3.5 miles one way
Elevation gain: 1,750 feet
Allow 2 to 2½ hours one way
Usually open July through September
High point: 10,350 feet
Topographic map:
U.S.G.S. Mt. Powell, Colo.
15′   1933

Two hikes described in this guide penetrate the wooded northeastern slopes of the Gore Range. Since the trailheads to Upper Cataract Lake (No. 23) at the base of Eagles Nest Mountain and Eaglesmere Lakes are only one-third mile apart and the Gore Range Trail connects the two main routes, you can combine the trips into a scenic loop. If you did the complete circuit from Eaglesmere Lakes to Upper Cataract Lake you would add 7.5 miles and 1,200 feet of elevation gain but you could save five miles and 700 feet of climbing by omitting the spur to Upper Cataract Lake. (Refer to the text and map of No. 23 for a description of this loop.)

One of the outstanding features of the climb to Eaglesmere Lakes is the impressive groves of aspen along the first half of the hike. However, other types of ground cover add variety, such as a section of sagebrush near the beginning, slopes of waist-high grass midway along the trek and dense stands of evergreens at the end. Carry drinking water as none is available along the route and take water purification tablets if you are backpacking.

From the south, drive on U.S. 6 (Interstate 70) to the junction of Colorado 9, one mile west of Dillon. Turn north and travel 17 miles to the side road to Heeney. Turn left, leaving the paved surface, and drive five miles to a sign indicating the spur to Cataract Creek and Gore-Eagles Nest Primitive Area. From the north, proceed on U.S. 40 to Kremmling and turn south onto Colorado 9. Travel 13 miles to a sign stating Green Mountain Reservoir and Heeney. Turn right, after two miles cross a dam and turn left. Continue along the road for three miles to the Wilderness spur road. Turn west and follow the dirt road for two miles to a fork 100 yards beyond the entrance to Cataract Creek Campground. Keep right and continue one-third mile to the end of the road at a parking and picnic area. The unsigned trail begins in an aspen grove at the west edge of the turnaround where a sign prohibiting motor vehicles is posted.

Walk along an old road for 250 yards to a gate. Continue through woods of large aspen trees and start climbing more noticeably. Curve left and traverse uphill along the slope. Near 0.5 mile travel through open sagebrush where you can look down onto Lower Cataract Lake. Farther along the route you will be able to see Tipperary Lake. Reenter woods and near 1.0 mile walk at a more gradual grade along a gently inclined slope. Pass through a second short stretch of sagebrush then resume hiking through aspen woods. As you gain elevation, tall sturdy evergreens begin to appear more prominently among the deciduous trees. For the next mile the trail travels through several meadows of tall grass and wild flowers that cling to the steep hillside.

After climbing through deep woods come to the junction of the Gore Range Trail at 2.8 miles. If you make the recommended loop on your return you will be following the trail that goes south. To reach Eaglesmere Lakes turn right and climb moderately for a short distance then walk at a more gradual grade with a few slight drops to the junction of the trail to Mahan Lake. Turn left and continue on the level for 200 yards to the first and smallest of the two Eaglesmere Lakes. Stay on the main trail to reach the narrow strip of land separating the lakes. Campsites are available here or at the south end of the larger lake.

Eaglesmere Lakes

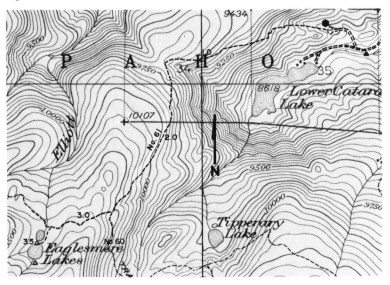

23 UPPER CATARACT LAKE

One day trip or backpack
Distance: 5.5 miles one way
Elevation gain: 2,350 feet, loss 250 feet
Allow 3½ to 4 hours one way
Usually open July through September
High point: 10,950 feet
Topographic map:
    U.S.G.S. Mt. Powell, Colo.
    15′   1933

Large Upper Cataract Lake lies below a steep rock wall at the base of Eagles Nest Mountain. The trail, which travels through woods during most of the climb, passes Surprise and Kat Lakes and you can extend the hike by continuing 1.5 miles beyond Upper Cataract Lake to Mirror Lake. A scenic loop is possible by heading northwest on the Gore Range Trail from the junction at 3.0 miles. This route winds through interesting rock formations then turns north and follows the trail described in the text for Eaglesmere Lakes (No. 22). This loop would add 2.5 miles and 350 feet of elevation gain and the short side trip to Eaglesmere Lakes would be only 1.4 miles longer with a negligible amount of climbing.

If you are approaching from the south, proceed on U.S. 6 (Interstate 70) to the junction of Colorado 9, one mile west of Dillon. Turn north and travel 17 miles to the side road to Heeney. Turn left, leaving the paved surface, and drive five miles to a sign indicating the spur to Cataract Creek and Gore-Eagles Nest Primitive Area. From the north, proceed on U.S. 40 to Kremmling and turn south onto Colorado 9. Travel 13 miles to a sign stating Green Mountain Reservoir and Heeney. Turn right, after two miles cross a dam and turn left. Continue along the road for three miles to the Wilderness spur road. Turn west and follow the dirt road for two miles to a fork 100 yards beyond the entrance to Cataract Creek Campground. Keep left and after a few hundred yards come to a large parking area on your left where a sign points to the beginning of the trail to Surprise Lake.

Cross Cataract Creek on a bridge and climb an open, grassy slope for several hundred feet before entering woods of aspen and a few evergreens. Continue uphill at a generally gentle grade and ford a shallow stream at 0.7 mile. Climb at a steeper, but steady, grade and eventually pass through several small open areas. Where a faint path goes left keep right as indicated by a sign pointing to Trail. The woods abruptly have become almost entirely composed of firs and the trail rises at a steeper angle. At 1.9 miles begin contouring southeast along the face of a wooded slope. Cross a small stream and one-quarter mile farther come to the junction of the Gore Range Trail. Turn right and after walking at a very gradual grade for one-tenth mile hike near the northern and northwestern side of Surprise Lake, traveling a short distance from the shore. A good resting place is near the northwest end and if you are there around early August you will be able to enjoy the yellow pond lily blossoms. Climb slightly from the lake then cross a stream and 150 yards beyond the easy ford come to a junction. If you make the recommended loop you will be taking the trail to the right on your return from Upper Cataract Lake.

Keep left on Trail 63 and continue through woods at a gradual grade for two miles then curve right and begin descending in switchbacks above Kat Lake. Come to the edge of a huge boulder field, wind down for several yards then traverse across the rocks 200 feet above the lake. Meet the junction of the spur to Kat Lake, turn left and after 200 yards come to the northeast shore of Upper Cataract Lake.

To make the recommended loop, return to the junction of the Gore Range Trail at 3.0 miles and turn left. Walk at a gradual downhill grade for one mile then begin dropping more noticeably to the junction of the spur to Tipperary Lake. Keep straight and wind down through an area of interesting rock formations. Cross turbulent Cataract Creek on a large bridge and, after descending for a short distance, begin climbing along an open slope. Then reenter woods and come to the junction of the trail to Eaglesmere Lakes. Keep straight to reach the lakes or turn right to finish the loop.

Kat Lake

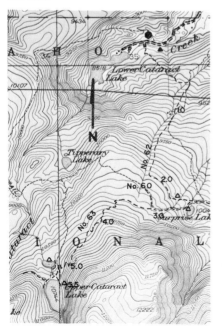

Indian Pond Lily at Surprise Lake

24 RAWAH LAKES

Backpack
Distance: 9 miles to Rawah Lake No. 1
Elevation gain: 2,600 feet, loss 380 feet
(Rawah Lake No. 1)
Allow 5½ to 6 hours one way
Usually open late June through September
High point: 11,250 feet
Topographic maps:
   U.S.G.S. Boston Peak, Colo.
   7.5′   1962
   U.S.G.S. Rawah Lakes, Colo.
   7.5′   1962

Four trails described in this guide penetrate the Rawah Wilderness, situated northwest of Rocky Mountain National Park in the heart of the Medicine Bow Range. The trail to Blue Lake (No. 27) enters the preserve from the south but the other three have a common trailhead near the eastern boundary and follow the same route for a few miles. The trail to West Branch Lakes (No. 26) goes southwest to a basin just above timberline and the trail to Camp Lakes (No. 25) traverses northward along the eastern boundary of the Wilderness.

Although all the hikes are through scenic terrain, the climb over 11,200 foot Grassy Pass to the Rawah Lakes traverses especially attractive country. In addition to the pleasing vistas, many varieties of wild flowers grow along the route and large gray rabbits frequent the slopes near the pass. Many side trips are possible, including climbs to Twin Crater Lakes and Bench Lake. The main trail continues beyond the lowest Rawah Lake to Sandbar and Camp Lakes.

Drive on Colorado 14 nine miles northeast of Cameron Pass or 19 miles west and south of the resort community of Idlewild to a sign indicating the road to Woods Landing. (The route over the pass is unpaved to a few miles east of this side road.) Turn north and proceed along the dirt road for six miles to a large parking area on the left side of the road 0.1 mile beyond the entrance to Tunnel Campground.

Walk to a sign south of the parking area and follow an old road that goes to the west.

After a short distance come to a sign pointing to Rawah Wilderness and turn left. Cross the West Branch of the Laramie River on a bridge and climb slightly to a fork where the path to the left drops to Tunnel Campground. Turn right and soon walk through an open area then enter a lovely aspen grove. Climb moderately along the wooded slope, switchbacking a few times, then descend to the register at the West Branch Drift Fence. A few hundred feet beyond the gate switchback and continue climbing at an irregular grade. Enter the Wilderness and at 2.4 miles come to the junction of the trail to Camp Lakes.

Keep left and walk at a very gradual grade for two-thirds mile to the footbridge over the North Fork of the Laramie River. Continue to the junction of the West Branch Trail. Turn right and climb at a moderate grade through deep woods. One mile from the junction cross two large streams. Although no foot bridges span the flows, the fords are not difficult. Switchback up, then hike at a gradual grade to the junction of the Twin Crater Lakes Trail at 5.0 miles. The route to these two lakes gains 650 feet of elevation in 1.2 miles. Keep right and soon begin dropping into an open grassy swale and at 5.8 miles ford a shallow stream. The faint route to Bench Lake heads southwest from this crossing. You can look down onto the lake from Grassy Pass if you want to study the terrain before making this side trip. Climb moderately through the meadows and clusters of trees toward the pass for one mile from the crossing then rise above timberline in two gradual switchbacks. Traverse up the slope to the pass.

Veer slighty left toward a large rock marker then traverse cross-country along the grassy slope at a moderate uphill grade, bearing very slighty left. You are aiming for a point just to the southwest of the low summit ahead to the north. Pass a tarn on your left and come to a level area. Continue across it for a short distance to a viewpoint 350 feet above Rawah Lake No. 3. The cross-country route to the cirque that holds Rawah Lake No. 4 heads southwest from here. If you want to continue the hike to the lower Rawah Lakes, descend north from the overlook on a trail along the west side of the low ridge above the lake.

Sign at trailhead

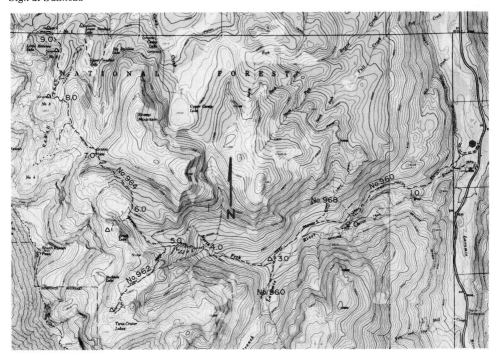

25 CAMP LAKES

One day trip or backpack
Distance: 8 miles one way
Elevation gain: 2,225 feet, loss 100 feet
Allow 4½ to 5½ hours one way
Usually open mid-June through September
High point: 10,725 feet
Topographic maps:
    U.S.G.S. Boston Peak, Colo.
    7.5'   **1962**
    U.S.G.S. Rawah Lakes, Colo.
    7.5'   **1962**

Two miles of the hike to Camp Lakes traverses along the bank of an abandoned water diversion canal near the eastern boundary of the Rawah Wilderness. The grassy shore at the lower of the two Camp Lakes is a good stopping place if you want a slightly shorter hike or backpack. From here you can continue one mile to Upper Camp Lake or you can make a side trip to Sandbar Lake or a short distance beyond the latter to the lowest of the Rawah Lakes. A long loop trip for backpackers would be possible by returning south from Rawah Lakes over Grassy Pass (No. 24). A few hundred yards of the route beyond 6.0 miles is faint.

Proceed on Colorado 14 nine miles northeast of Cameron Pass or 19 miles west and south of the resort community of Idlewild to a sign indicating the road to Woods Landing. (The route over the pass is unpaved to a few miles east of this side road.) Turn north and drive along the dirt road for six miles to a large parking area on the left side of the road 0.1 mile beyond the entrance to Tunnel Campground.

Walk to a sign south of the parking area and follow an old road that goes to the west. After a short distance come to a sign pointing to Rawah Wilderness and turn left. Cross the West Branch of the Laramie River on a bridge and climb a short distance to a fork where the path to the left drops to Tunnel Campground. Turn right and soon walk through an open area then enter a lovely aspen grove. During mid-summer assorted wild flowers grow in the grass beneath the trees. Beyond the junction at 2.2 miles, climb slightly and make one set of short switchbacks. Resume traversing at a moderate but not steady grade to a second set of switchbacks and continue traveling uphill. Drop slightly to the register at the West Branch Drift Fence. A few hundred feet beyond the gate switchback for a third time and continue climbing along the wooded slope. Soon after crossing a good sized stream come to the Wilderness boundary and 0.2 mile farther come to the junction of the trail to Rawah and West Branch Lakes (No's. 24 and 26).

Turn right, climb steeply for 120 yards, and where you come to an open area turn right. Traverse for 0.1 mile along a winding path then curve left and pass a cabin. Resume climbing steeply through woods. Cross a small stream at 3.0 miles and one-half mile farther come to a level area where you will have a view of the peaks above the West Branch drainage. Again start to climb, pass the remains of a building on your left and come to the ditch. Walk beside the canal at an almost level grade for two miles to a point where the ditch curves to the right and traverses to the east along an open slope. Turn left and follow the obvious, but unsigned, path that heads west up the slope.

Climb gradually through an area of grass and clumps of evergreens. About 0.3 mile from the ditch, where the trail begins to drop and become faint, veer slightly right and walk through a small meadow to a band of trees. Then go through a second strip of grass to the woods on the far side. Although not obvious, a blaze has been cut into one of the trees. Resume hiking on a well-defined path and descend slightly to the junction of the unmaintained trail that follows the ditch around the face of the ridge. Turn left and hike at an almost level grade for about one-half mile to an open area. Curve left to the southeastern shore of Camp Lake.

To reach Upper Camp Lake, travel around the southern edge of the lower lake to the junction of the trail to Sandbar and the Rawah Lakes. Turn left and climb for three-quarters mile, gaining 280 feet, to the larger of the two lakes in the basin.

Looking west at the beginning of the canal

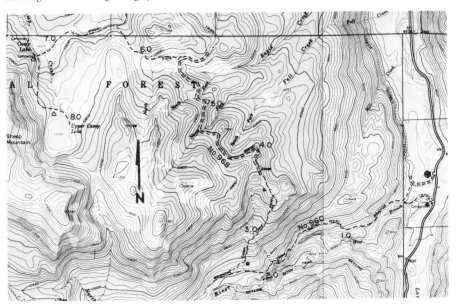

26 WEST BRANCH LAKES

One day trip or backpack
Distance: 6.5 miles one way
Elevation gain: 2,540 feet
Allow 3½ to 4½ hours one way
Usually open mid-June through September
High point: 11,140 feet
Topographic maps:
    U.S.G.S. Boston Peak, Colo.
    7.5'   1962
    U.S.G.S. Rawah Lakes, Colo.
    7.5'   1962

Like the trip to Rawah Lakes (No. 24), the hike to the basin holding Island and Carey Lakes and the several tarns at the headwaters of the West Branch of the Laramie River travels through attractive woods and large meadows before climbing above timberline to the tundra of the highlands. Much time can be spent in easy explorations among the lakes within the cirque or you can make a short but strenuous side trip to Blue Lake (No. 27) that would add a total of three miles and 1,200 feet of elevation gain. Campsites are especially plentiful in the meadows between 3.8 and 4.9 miles.

Drive on Colorado 14 nine miles northeast of Cameron Pass or 19 miles west and south of the resort community of Idlewild to a sign indicating the road to Woods Landing. (The route over the pass is unpaved to a few miles east of this side road.) Turn north and proceed along the dirt road for six miles to a large parking area on the left side of the road 0.1 mile beyond the entrance to Tunnel Campground.

Walk to a sign south of the parking area and follow an old road that goes to the west. After a short distance come to a sign pointing to Rawah Wilderness and turn left. Cross the West Branch of the Laramie River on a bridge and climb a short distance to a fork where the path to the left drops to Tunnel Campground. Turn right and soon walk through an open area then enter an aspen grove. Climb slightly and make one set of short switchbacks. Continue traversing at a moderate but not steady grade to a second set of switchbacks and continue uphill. As you gain elevation, evergreens gradually replace the aspen. Drop to the register at the West Branch Drift Fence. A few hun-

dred feet beyond the gate switchback for a third time and continue climbing along the wooded slope. Soon after crossing a good sized stream come to the Wilderness boundary and 0.2 mile farther come to the junction of the trail to Camp Lakes (No. 25).

Keep left and walk at a very gradual grade for two-thirds mile to the footbridge over the North Fork of the Laramie River several feet upstream from the horse crossing. Return to the main trail, pass a sign pointing right to an outhouse and 150 yards from the crossing come to the junction of the trail to the Rawah Lakes. Keep left and climb through attractive woods. Cross a few small side streams and climb more noticeably then level off and one mile from the junction traverse through a meadow. Hike at a moderate grade through a wooded area then come to a large complex of clearings. At 4.9 miles, near the south end of the meadows, come to the junction of the trail to Blue Lake. If you plan to make this side trip, turn left, cross the creek and climb steeply to the pass above Blue Lake.

To continue to Island Lake, keep straight at the junction. Soon after reentering woods make a short set of switchbacks. Ford a stream and a short distance farther cross a second creek, going downstream to locate a log spanning the flow. The grade increases and the woods become less dense. Walk at a gradual grade for several hundred feet then resume climbing along slopes covered with grass, wild flowers and scattered trees. The trail rises above timberline and eventually stops. Note landmarks so you can locate the return path. To reach Island Lake, the largest of the group, bear left and climb for 0.4 mile to the head of the cirque.

Camp on the West Branch

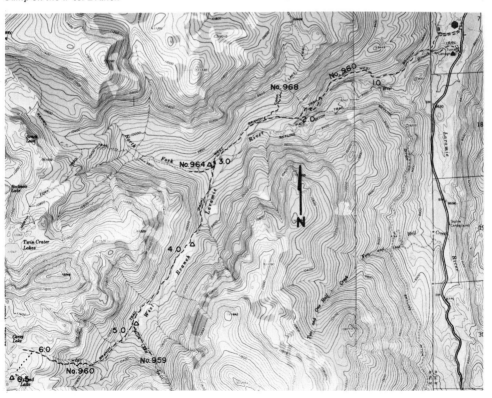

27 BLUE LAKE

One day trip or backpack
Distance: 5 miles one way
Elevation gain: 1,600 feet, loss 100 feet
Allow 2½ to 3 hours one way
Usually open mid-June through September
High point: 10,820 feet
Topographic maps:
   U.S.G.S. Chambers Lake, Colo.
   7.5'   1962
   U.S.G.S. Clark Peak, Colo.
   7.5'   1962

The hike to Blue Lake, situated in the southern part of the Rawah Wilderness, begins at Chambers Lake, a popular spot for boating and fishing, and climbs through woods to timberline. If you are doing the hike as a backpack or want a more strenuous one day trip you can continue along the main trail beyond Blue Lake to the junction with the West Branch Trail then climb to scenic Island and Carey Lakes (No. 26). This side trip would add a total of six miles and 2,300 feet of elevation gain.

Proceed on Colorado 14 seven miles northeast of Cameron Pass or twenty-one miles west and south of the resort community of Idlewild to the entrance to the campground at Chambers Lake on the northwest side of the highway. The road is unpaved over the pass and to a point several miles northeast of Chambers Lake. Turn northwest and follow the sign that indicates the way to Blue Lake trailhead and parking lot located at the northwest edge of the campground. The trailhead is marked by a large diagrammatic sign.

After a few yards descend to a large bridge over Wright Creek. Keep straight for several feet beyond the span then turn right and travel beside the shore of Chambers Lake for 0.2 mile before veering left into the woods. Rise slightly then drop to the bridge over Fall Creek. Climb steeply in switchbacks then travel through woods at a more moderate grade above the creek. Cross an old road, pass a register and at 2.1 miles enter the Rawah Wilderness. The grade becomes more gradual and the route climbs and drops slightly as it crosses several small side streams.

Near 4.0 miles pass through a small meadow and cross a creek on a pole bridge then resume winding up through woods. Two-thirds mile from the crossing climb an open slope and walk on the level along a narrow bench with a steep grassy incline rising above to your left and a rim of trees on the right. At the end of this corridor where you are above the southwest end of Blue Lake turn right, leaving the trail, and drop to the level of the shore. To find a good camping spot walk through woods to a point midway along the south side and several yards from the water's edge.

The main trail continues traversing the open slope above Blue Lake then climbs over a low pass before dropping steeply to the crossing of the West Branch of the Laramie River and the junction of the West Branch Trail.

Blue Lake

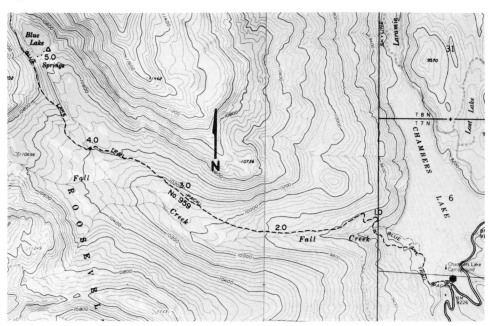

28 SHADOW MOUNTAIN LOOKOUT

One day trip
Distance: 4.3 miles one way
Elevation gain: 1,525 feet
Allow 2½ to 3 hours one way
Usually open June through September
High point: 9,923 feet
Topographic map:
  U.S.G.S. Shadow Mountain, Colo.
  7.5′   1958

The lookout

From the walkway around the tall stone and wood lookout tower on Shadow Mountain you will be able to see north up the Kawuneeche Valley to the Never Summer Range, southwest to the Gore Range and far to the south over less mountainous terrain. The only source of drinking water along the hike is a creek at 3.4 miles.

The lakes visible below the lookout serve as the west side reservoirs for the Big Thompson Project, an extensive system to provide farmers on the east side of the Front Range with water for irrigation. Water is pumped from Lake Granby up to Shadow Mountain Lake then up to Grand Lake, the only natural lake of the three. From the northeast end of Grand Lake the water flows through the 13.1 mile long Alva B. Adams Tunnel under the southern portion of Rocky Mountain National Park to the eastern slope then through a series of conduits, tunnels, penstocks and powerplants to two reservoirs. Begun in 1937, the system was completed in 1958.

Drive on U.S. 40 to the west end of Granby and turn north on U.S. 34. Proceed 14 miles to the junction with Colorado 278: keep right and follow the sign to Grand Lake and Village. After one-third mile curve right at a fork, again following the sign to Grand Lake, and about 0.5 mile farther turn right onto Vine Street where a sign indicates the route to Daven Haven Lodge. After 100 yards turn right then follow the winding main road for 0.5 mile to a junction. Turn left, cross a bridge over a canal and continue one-quarter mile to a sign reading Dead End Road. The last available parking is off the road to the left here. If these few spaces are filled, drive back to another turnoff.

Walk up the main road (not the one that goes right to private property) for 0.1 mile to a sign stating East Shore Trail and listing several mileages, about 75 feet off the lake side of the road. Climb, then drop for a few yards and travel near the wooded shore of Grand Lake, walking generally on the level. Near 1.2 miles travel away from the lake and come to the junction of the trail to Shadow Mountain Dam.

Keep left and after a few yards begin traversing up a wooded slope at a steady, moderate grade. About 0.5 mile from the junction switchback to the left and come to a ridge top. Curve left and walk along the narrow crest where you occasionally will be able to see the lookout. Continue climbing through woods and curve right where the ridge you have been following merges with a larger slope. Rise moderately past an area where several small ridges radiate downslope. Travel on the level then resume climbing and pass beneath a knob of rock outcroppings. Walk north, traveling along the slope of a side canyon, then at its head curve right and traverse the opposite wall.

At the end of this long, straight stretch come to Sanger Creek and switchback up to the left. Climb in short switchbacks for one-half mile to a saddle. Turn left, walk along the crest for a short distance then wind up a hump to the lookout. A cluster of rocks to the north of the building affords a good place to enjoy your lunch. The actual summit of Shadow Mountain is three-quarters mile to the southeast. Outbuildings are downslope from the hitching rail several yards before the lookout.

Rock formations above the trail

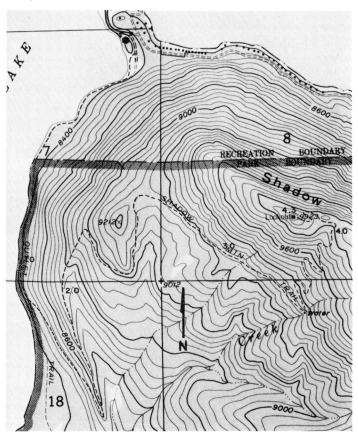

29 LAKE VERNA

One day trip or backpack
Distance: 7 miles one way
Elevation gain: 1,850 feet
Allow 4 to 4½ hours one way
Usually open July through September
High point: 10,200 feet
Topographic maps:
   U.S.G.S. McHenrys Peak, Colo.
   7.5'   1957
   U.S.G.S. Shadow Mountain, Colo.
   7.5'   1958

For almost its entire length the trail follows along Grand Lake's East Inlet Creek as it winds through woods, large meadows and valleys, and drops over rock bands. Another trip, (No. 30), follows North Inlet Creek that also empties into Grand Lake. The route passes Lone Pine Lake at 5.0 miles and cross-country side trips can be made beyond Lake Verna to Spirit and Fourth Lakes. During periods of wet weather or early in the season the ground at the campsites around Lake Verna can be very damp so during these times overnight stays may be more comfortable at Lone Pine Lake.

Proceed on U.S. 40 to the west end of Granby and turn north on U.S. 34. Drive 14 miles to the junction with Colorado 278: keep right, and follow the sign to Grand Lake and Village. After one-third mile the road forks. Keep left, as indicated by the sign pointing to the Big Thompson Irrigation Tunnel, and travel 2.4 miles to a sign stating Adams Falls Trailhead Parking. Keep left and after 200 yards enter a large parking area marked by a sign identifying the East Inlet Trail.

Walk up the old road bed that heads east from the parking area for several yards then curve south, passing outbuildings, to the register. Climb through woods for 0.3 mile to a sign pointing right to Adams Falls, only a few hundred feet off the trail to the south. Although the same surname is used for both the Falls and the irrigation tunnel near the trailhead, these features actually were named for two different men. Jay Adams built three houses on Grand Lake and the Falls were named for him in 1917. The Alva B. Adams Tunnel honors the Colorado Senator who did much to secure the Big Thompson Project.

Keep left on the main trail and climb slightly to the boundary of Rocky Mountain National Park. Walk on the level beside East Inlet Creek then travel in woods near the edge of a meadow. Between 1.0 and 1.5 miles hike above a second, larger meadow. Continue up moderately, at one point passing under blasted rocks, then traverse a steep, wooded slope. Make one short set of switchbacks before walking along the base of a rock band. Climb more steeply then wind up around rocks to the crest where you can look back down over the valley.

Drop slightly into a swale of boulders and trees, climb a short distance then descend over slabs toward East Inlet Creek. The trail curves sharply to the left a few yards before the stream and travels on the level through woods. Climb at a generally moderate grade and eventually pass a sign identifying the Mt. Cairns campsite. Wind up and after a more moderate stretch cross a bridge at the base of a rock wall. Switchback steeply a few times then hike at an irregular grade to a bridge over East Inlet Creek. Climb several yards from the span to the junction of the trail to Paradise Park. Keep left and wind up through woods for 0.8 mile to the south shore of Lone Pine Lake.

The main trail curves right, passes an outbuilding on your right and continues near the southeastern end of the lake. Cross a scree slope of large boulders then begin winding up through woods, crossing several bridges over small streams. At the end of the final span turn sharply right and traverse along a rocky wall. Enter the upper portion of the boulder field you crossed earlier then turn left into a steep-sided little valley. Travel at a slight uphill grade just above East Inlet Creek. Farther on, rock slides and log jams have dammed the flow of the stream and formed ponds. Continue through deeper woods then drop briefly to the tip of Lake Verna. The trail continues around the north side to the eastern end of the lake.

Gorge on East Inlet Creek

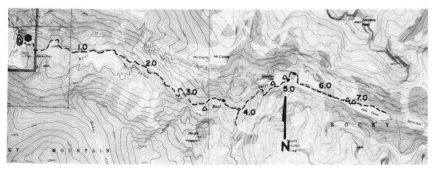

30 LAKES NOKONI AND NANITA

Backpack
Distance: 10 miles one way
Elevation gain: 2,580 feet, loss 300 feet
Allow 5½ to 6½ hours one way
Usually open July through September
High point: 11,080 feet
Topographic maps:
    U.S.G.S. Grand Lake, Colo.
    7.5'   1958
    U.S.G.S. McHenrys Peak, Colo.
    7.5'   1957

Many places in Colorado are named for Indians or use Indian words that describe some characteristic of the feature. The two lakes visited at the end of this scenic trek through woods and meadows are an example — Nokoni was one of the leading chiefs of the Comanche tribe and Nanita was either a Navajo word meaning plains Indians or the word used by a tribe of Texas Indians for the Comanches.

These two lakes, situated in cirques near timberline, are separated by a 300 foot high ridge. Although long, the trail never climbs steeply and many sections are almost level.

Drive on U.S. 40 to the west end of Granby and turn north on U.S. 34. Proceed 14 miles to the junction with Colorado 278: keep right, following the sign to Grand Lake and Village. After one-third mile the road forks. Keep left, as indicated by the sign pointing to the Big Thompson Irrigation Tunnel, and continue three-quarters mile to a marker on your left pointing to the Tonahutu Creek and North Inlet Trails. You can park along the shoulder or turn left, drive up the road, keeping left where it forks after 75 yards, and continue 200 yards to a signed parking area on the left.

Walk along the road 200 feet beyond the parking area to a sign on your right stating North Inlet Trail. Drop for 75 feet and cross a large bridge at the boundary of Rocky Mountain National Park. Descend along the road bed through woods then level off and walk along the edge of a large meadow. Reenter woods then at 1.3 miles pass through an open area with picnic tables and outbuildings. Continue along the road for 150 yards to the guard station. A large sign just beyond the buildings lists several mileages and identifies the beginning of the trail proper.

The trail travels through woods at a gradual grade and at one point passes near a meadow. Near 3.0 miles begin climbing more noticeably and after traversing up a rocky slope come to a sign marking the path to Cascade Falls. Keep on the main trail and several hundred yards farther pass a large campsite on your right. Climb moderately for a short distance then walk near the edge of a large meadow. Cross a small scree slope that houses a colony of conies then resume walking through woods. Near 4.1 miles climb in one switchback then walk briefly on the level before descending for a short distance. Wind above the gorges formed by turbulent North Inlet Creek and begin heading in an easterly direction. Hike at a moderate grade through woods and at 6.1 miles pass a large pond and meadow on your right.

Come to a small stream and several yards farther cross Ptarmigan Creek on a foot log. Begin climbing more noticeably and make one short set of switchbacks. After a moderate uphill stretch make a second set and continue for one-half mile to the junction of the trail to Flattop Mountain. Farther along the hike you will be able to see the long, level summit of this mountain and also the pyramid shape of Hallett Peak.

Keep right, drop slightly, then cross North Inlet Creek on a large bridge. Turn left and follow beside the stream for a short distance before curving right. Traverse along a wooded valley wall for one-third mile then begin a series of long switchbacks, coming at one point to an overlook at the edge of the deep gorge below Lake Nokoni. Climb along the steep, rocky wall of the canyon then curve right and walk through woods for a short distance to a flat area just before the shore where a sign points right to camping areas. To reach Lake Nanita turn left, cross the outlet creek and climb up then down the rocky ridge to the lake.

Early fall mushrooms at Lake Granby

Clark's Nutcracker

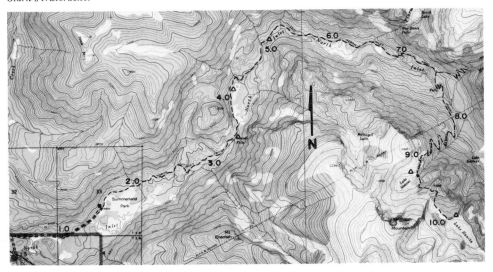

31 LAKE OF THE CLOUDS

One day trip or backpack
Distance: 6.3 miles one way
Elevation gain: 2,430 feet
Allow 4 to 4½ hours one way
Usually open July through September
High point: 11,430 feet
Topographic maps:
U.S.G.S. Fall River Pass, Colo.
7.5′   1958
U.S.G.S. Mount Richthofen, Colo.
7.5′   1957

Lake of the Clouds derives its name from the four peaks along the crest of the Never Summer Range, which are named after four different types of cloud formations — Mounts Cirrus, Cumulus, Nimbus and Stratus. However, the lake rests in a basin well above timberline on the northeastern slope of Howard Mountain. Luke Howard, an early 19th Century English meteorologist, was the first to classify cloud formations and his name would have been a whimsically erudite choice for the peak. Most likely the mountain was named for a miner who worked in the area during the early 1880's.

The final 0.5 mile of the hike is over a massive boulder field and an easily negotiated but steep slope. Although much more demanding than hiking along a trail, no special climbing skills are needed for this section.

Proceed on U.S. 34 ten miles north of the Grand Lake Entrance to Rocky Mountain National Park or ten miles southwest from the Visitor Center at Fall River Pass to a sign stating Phantom Valley Trailhead. Turn west and drive down the side road for 0.1 mile to a fork. Keep left, as indicated by the sign pointing to Red Mountain Trail, and enter a parking area.

Cross the North Fork of the Colorado River on a foot bridge and walk 200 feet through a clearing to the western wall of the valley then begin climbing gradually through woods. After three-quarters mile cross an open, rocky slope where you can look down on a portion of the Kawuneeche Valley. (This name is a corrupted spelling of the Arapaho word for coyote.) Reenter woods and at 1.2 miles curve north and wind up at a moderate, but uneven, grade occasionally passing through rocky or small open areas. Begin a very gradual descent and come to an overlook where you will be able to see down to the parking area. Continue downhill to the crossing of Opposition Creek then resume climbing. The grade increases considerably just before reaching the Grand Ditch.

Turn right and walk along the road that parallels the canal. The digging of this 14 mile agricultural irrigation channel was started in the late 1800's and the system still is maintained. Just beyond Lost Creek at 3.5 miles you will be able to look down onto the large meadow near the head of the Kawuneeche Valley, the site of Lulu City (see No. 32). About two miles beyond where you first met the road, be watching for a large bridge across the canal at Dutch Creek. (The span may be moved to the side of the Ditch soon after Labor Day, but a ford is not difficult that late in the season.) Climb through woods and soon pass the remains of two cabins. The grade becomes more moderate and the route continues winding up beneath conifers. Pass through a small meadow with a stream flowing through it and a short distance farther walk along the shore of a tarn situated at the south end of a larger meadow. A campsite is located in the woods near the west edge of the clearing.

Resume the winding ascent and soon begin climbing more steeply At the edge of the timber turn right and traverse up a low rocky bluff toward a large cairn. At the crest, where the trail ends, turn left (southwest) toward a 400 foot high rock wall with a waterfall running down its face. This flow is the outlet from Lake of the Clouds. Descend over the boulder field, generally aiming for the grassy shelves on the wall to the right of the falls. Where you resume climbing head toward the left hand edge of the benches, just above where the outlet begins to flow underground. Turn right and keep on the lower ledges until the slope ahead begins to fall away. Turn left and resume climbing steeply toward the crest. At the edge of the basin walk several hundred feet over grass and slabs to the shore of the lake.

Boulder field below the lake

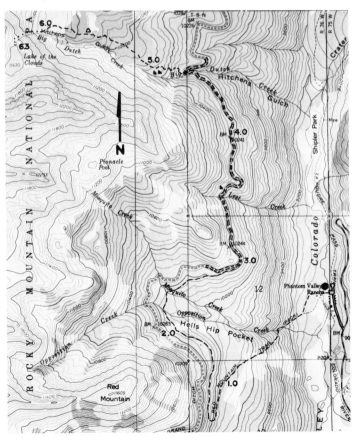

32 THUNDER PASS

One day trip or backpack
Distance: 6.5 miles one way
Elevation gain: 2,580 feet, loss 250 feet
Allow 3½ to 4½ hours one way
Usually open July through September
High point: 11,331 feet
Topographic map:
    U.S.G.S. Fall River Pass, Colo.
    7.5'   1958

Lulu City, passed midway along the climb to Thunder Pass, was founded in 1879 and by 1882 had a population of 500 miners, shopkeepers and their families. The following year it was a ghost town, a victim of falling gold prices. Today, the remnants of a few log cabins mark the site. Another reminder of earlier times is the faint old wagon road the trail follows for portions of the trek. This road went north through the Kawuneeche Valley, over Thunder Pass, down past Michigan Lakes to Walden.

The entire trail is pleasing visually as well as interesting historically. Thunder Pass is a large, rolling open crest and affords good views to the north and west. A scenic loop trip that would add only a few feet of elevation gain and 2.5 miles can be made by walking along the Grand Ditch for 2.5 miles then descending along the rim of Little Yellowstone Canyon on the trail from La Poudre Pass (No. 33).

The only campsites are at the Michigan Lakes outside the Park boundary.

Drive on U.S. 34 ten miles north of the Grand Lake entrance to Rocky Mountain National Park or ten miles southwest from the Visitor Center at Fall River Pass to a sign stating Phantom Valley Trailhead. Turn west and proceed down the side road for 0.1 mile to a fork. Keep right, following the sign pointing to Lulu City, and enter a large parking area. A sign at the north edge of the turnaround stating La Poudre Pass Trail and listing several mileages identifies the beginning of the hike.

Walk along the grass, brush and tree-covered floor of the valley, traveling beside the North Fork of the Colorado River for a short distance, then traverse the base of the valley wall. The grade is a series of level stretches interspersed with short sections of moderate ups and downs. Near 1.0 mile pass the remains of the two Shipler cabins, enter deeper woods and travel along a faint road bed. Curve gradually northeast and climb at a more steady grade. Come to the junction of the trail to La Poudre Pass. (If you make the recommended loop, you will be returning along this trail.)

Turn left and begin descending moderately, eventually switchbacking a few times. The trail becomes level and passes through a large meadow, the site of Lulu City. A short distance from the north end of the clearing keep left (straight) where the trail forks. (The path to the right climbs to meet the trail to La Poudre Pass.) Curve around the base of the low ridge and walk at river level before crossing the flow on a bridge. Travel along a rocky portion of the former stream bed then go up through a little canyon. Enter deeper woods and after a short climb come to the junction of another connector to the La Poudre Pass Trail. Keep left and continue uphill steeply. Eventually, the grade becomes more moderate and one mile from the junction above the bridge the trail comes to a wide, smooth road. The route, marked by a cairn, resumes on the opposite side a short distance to the right. Walk through a small meadow then climb for several yards to the road that parallels the Grand Ditch.

Cross the canal on a bridge and walk for a short distance along the old road bed at an almost level grade before climbing more noticeably. One-half mile from the Ditch go through the center of a large meadow. Reenter woods at the opposite side of the clearing and climb more steeply. After another 0.5 mile abruptly leave the forest and begin traversing up an open slope. Switchback to the right and continue up along the faint roadbed. Enter the small valley below the pass, wind through the swale at a very moderate grade then make the final, short climb to the crest at the Park boundary. The dirt road winds down to the Michigan Lakes just below the pass. The jagged crest of the Nokhu Crags pokes the sky to the northwest and the Medicine Bow Range fills much of the scene to the north.

Remains of Lulu City

Static Peak

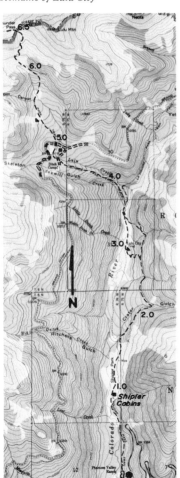

33 LA POUDRE PASS

One day trip or backpack
Distance: 7 miles one way
Elevation gain: 1,285 feet, loss 100 feet
Allow 4 to 4½ hours one way
Usually open late June through September
High point: 10,186 feet
Topographic map:
   U.S.G.S. Fall River Pass, Colo.
   7.5'   1958

Unlike most passes, La Poudre Pass is a long, flat-bottomed, meadow-filled valley. In fact, its earlier name was Mountain Meadows Pass. Scenically, the most impressive part of the hike is the 1.5 mile section above the fantastic rock formations of Little Yellowstone Canyon. Man-made remains can be seen by making a short side trip to Lulu City, for three years a busy mining town that once supported 500 people. A loop trip that would add 2.5 miles and less than 200 feet of elevation gain is possible by returning along the Thunder Pass Trail (No. 32).

Proceed on U.S. 34 ten miles north of the Grand Lake Entrance to Rocky Mountain National Park or ten miles southwest from the Visitor Center at Fall River Pass to a sign stating Phantom Valley Trailhead. Turn west and drive down the side road for 0.1 mile to a fork. Keep right, following the sign pointing to Lulu City, and enter a large parking area. A sign at the north edge of the turnaround stating La Poudre Pass Trail and listing several mileages identifies the beginning of the hike.

Walk along the grass, brush and tree covered floor of the valley, traveling beside the North Fork of the Colorado River for a short distance, then traverse the base of the valley wall. The grade is a series of level stretches interspersed with short sections of moderate ups and downs. Near 1.0 mile pass the remains of the two Shipler cabins. Joe Shipler was the first miner to settle in the valley. The main cabin, built in 1876, was occupied until 1914 and its sod roof did not collapse until 1963. Enter deeper woods and travel along a faint road bed. Curve gradually northeast and climb at a more steady grade. Come to the junction of the trail that goes down past Lulu City and climbs to Thunder Pass. (If you make the recom-

mended loop, you will return along this trail.)

Keep right and soon begin a very gradual descent. Weave in and out of little side canyons and during one stretch the large meadow that was the site of the once-thriving Lulu City can be seen below. Pass an unmarked downhill path on your left that meets the Thunder Pass Trail just north of Lulu City. Keep right, drop gradually to river level and walk near the flow before crossing it on foot bridges. Turn right and pass a sign identifying the beginning of Little Yellowstone Canyon. For the next several hundred yards the trail travels through extremely dense timber. Pass the junction of a second connecting path to the Thunder Pass Trail, keep right and cross a small stream on log foot bridges.

Climb at a moderate, steady grade, eventually coming close to the rim of the canyon. Cross the severely eroded ravine formed by Lady Creek on a bridge supported by a tall stone pillar and continue up along the wooded slope. Go in and out of a canyon and traverse a barren slope for a short distance. The grade lessens and the trail enters a second, larger canyon. Cross a creek at its head and drop slightly as you walk along the south facing slope. Travel almost on the level around the face of a ridge to the rim of the third and largest canyon. Leave the trail and walk a few feet toward the edge for a good view.

Continue uphill at a steady grade then cross a small stream and begin a series of switchbacks. Wind up through an area of small clearings before climbing steeply for a short distance to the road that parallels the Grand Ditch. Turn right and follow the Ditch for 1.6 miles to the south end of La Poudre Pass where a bridge crosses the canal. A ranger station and a path to the campsites are on the opposite side of the span.

To make the recommended loop, return to the point where you first met the road and continue in a southwesterly direction beside the Ditch for 2.5 miles. A few hundred feet beyond a cluster of buildings come to a foot bridge across the canal. Look for an unmarked trail across the road and follow it. (Refer to Trail No. 32 for a map and detailed information for the remainder of the hike.)

Little Yellowstone Canyon

34 SPECIMEN MOUNTAIN

One day trip
Distance: 3 miles one way
Elevation gain: 1,740 feet
Allow 2 to 2½ hours one way
Usually open July through September
High point: 12,489 feet
Topographic map:
   U.S.G.S. Fall River Pass, Colo.
   7.5′   1958

The saddle at 1.5 miles is one of the best vantage points in Rocky Mountain National Park for spotting bighorn sheep. Even if you are not fortunate enough to see any of these agile animals, you will be surrounded by scenic terrain along the trek. Two-thirds of the climb is above timberline and during the ascent you will have good views of the Never Summer Range. Looking northwest from the narrow summit you can study the jagged spires of the Nokhu Crags (also called the Seven Utes) and beyond them to a portion of North Park. Closer to the southwest is the Fall River Pass Visitor Center and the western portion of Trail Ridge Road above timberline and Longs Peak caps the skyline in the distance. Turning to the southwest, you may be able to see as far as the Gore Range.

The trail climbs very steeply for much of its distance and no water is available at the trailhead or along the hike.

Drive on Trail Ridge Road (U.S. 34) 16 miles north of the Grand Lake Entrance of Rocky Mountain National Park or four miles southwest from the Visitor Center at Fall River Pass to a parking area on the north side of the highway a short distance southwest from the outlet end of Poudre Lake.

The trail (may be unmarked) rises from the northwest side of the turnout through a grassy, open slope for several hundred feet to the register. Curve right and begin climbing very steeply through woods. Periodically, the trail grade moderates, but usually the route rises abruptly. Leave the timber at 1.1 miles and begin a more gradual traverse along the tundra. Your destination is the most northerly of the two peaks visible from the open slope. Four-tenths mile beyond timberline come to a saddle at the base of the first peak where interesting rock formations frame the view of the Never Summer Range to the west. The composition of the rocks here is evidence of the volcanic origin of Specimen Mountain. Interestingly, the English translation for the Indian name of the peak is "Mountain Smokes." Bighorn sheep frequently graze on the western side of the summit ridge and you may be able to spot some by studying carefully the slopes below the saddle.

Turn right and climb steeply near the rim. After the first pitch the grade moderates somewhat. Cross the top of the lower peak, cross a short rocky stretch and continue dropping gradually to a saddle. Climb the final 300 feet along the narrow ridge to the summit. Walk on the level for several yards to reach the cairn and metal tube containing the summit register.

Rain over the Never Summer Range

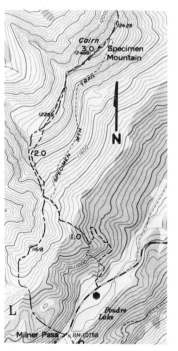

Summit of Specimen Mountain

35 YPSILON LAKE

One day trip or backpack
Distance: 5 miles one way
Elevation gain: 2,085 feet, loss 200 feet
Allow 3 to 3½ hours one way
Usually open July through September
High point: 10,710 feet
Topographic map:
    U.S.G.S. Trail Ridge, Colo.
    7.5'   1957

Aspen leaves near the Roaring River

Ypsilon is Greek for the letter Y and when viewed from a distance the long, snow-filled erosion channels centered on the southeast face of Ypsilon Mountain unmistakably have this outline. Although sharing the name of the peak, Ypsilon Lake actually perches on a bench several hundred feet below timberline. For a closer view of the mountain amid more scenic terrain you can make the strenuous cross-country side trip to the Spectacle Lakes. This climb involves an additional one-half mile and 800 feet of elevation gain.

Proceed on Trail Ridge Road (U.S. 34) 1.9 miles west of the Fall River Entrance to Rocky Mountain National Park or 1.5 miles north of Deer Ridge Junction to the sign identifying Fall River Road and parking for the Lawn Lake Trailhead. (Deer Ridge Junction is 2.8 miles west of the Beaver Meadows Entrance.) Turn north and after several hundred feet turn right and continue to the parking area where a small sign gives the mileages to Ypsilon and Lawn Lakes.

The trail begins at a large bulletin board and, although the path rises steeply for the first few hundred feet, the grade soon moderates. Where two trails join, first on the right then the left, continue climbing on the main route. After two sets of switchbacks resume traversing northwest along the wooded slope

above Horseshoe Park. Near 0.5 mile begin curving into the side canyon formed by the Roaring River. Hike at a gradual grade then drop slightly to the junction of the trail to Lawn and Crystal Lakes (No. 36).

Turn left and descend to the bridge across the Roaring River. Walk on the level in a northerly direction for a few hundred yards then switchback left and traverse up the slope at a steep grade. Cross a level area where you will be able to look down on the Sheep Lakes and Horseshoe Park. Resume climbing at a steeper grade and hike for one mile up a narrow, wooded ridge crest. The grade becomes more moderate and the trail winds through less dense woods for 1.5 miles before traversing downhill for a few dozen yards to little Chipmunk Lake. Wend your way around boulders and trees and after a very short up and down across an open, rocky swath climb slightly before the final, steep descent to Ypsilon Lake. Cross the inlet creek to reach the numbered campsites.

If you plan to make the very steep climb to the Spectacle Lakes, follow the inlet creek to Ypsilon Lake up to the outlet stream from the lower Spectacle Lake. Cross the flows and climb steeply along the west side of the outlet for about one-quarter mile to the first lake.

Falls at Ypsilon Lake

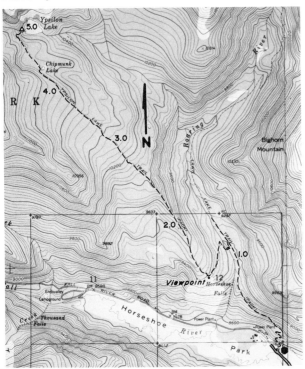

36 LAWN AND CRYSTAL LAKES

One day trip or backpack
Distance: 7.5 miles one way
Elevation gain: 2,900 feet
Allow 4½ to 5 hours one way
Usually open July through September
High point: 11,550 feet
Topographic maps:
    U.S.G.S. Estes Park, Colo.
    7.5′   1961
    U.S.G.S. Trail Ridge, Colo.
    7.5′   1957

Crystal Lake, situated in the north central portion of Rocky Mountain National Park, is the headwaters of the Roaring River and, except for the first one-half mile, the entire hike follows beside or near this turbulent flow. Although always scenic, the trail along the wooded slopes above the river is not as impressive as the final 1.5 miles between Lawn and Crystal Lakes. This latter section winds up over tundra to a basin filled with huge boulders and a cluster of tarns.

Drive on Trail Ridge Road (U.S. 34) one mile west of the Fall River Entrance to Rocky Mountain National Park or 1.5 miles north of Deer Ridge Junction to the sign identifying Fall River Road and parking for the Lawn Lake Trailhead. (Deer Ridge Junction is 2.8 miles west of the Beaver Meadows Entrance.) Turn north and after several hundred feet turn right and continue to the parking area where a small sign gives the mileages to Ypsilon and Lawn Lakes.

The trail begins at a large bulletin board and, although the path rises steeply for the first few hundred feet, the grade moderates. Where two trails join, first on the right then the left, continue climbing on the main route. After two sets of switchbacks traverse to the northwest on the wooded slope above

Horseshoe Park. Near 0.5 mile begin curving into the side canyon formed by the Roaring River. Hike at a gradual grade then drop slightly to the junction of the trail to Ypsilon Lake (No. 35).

Keep right and continue walking at a very moderate grade near the Roaring River through both pure and mixed stands of aspen and conifers. As the grade increases the direction of travel changes gradually to the northeast. Just after crossing a small stream near 3.0 miles curve right and begin a long switchback. During the next mile the trail makes four sets of switchbacks.

Traverse along the valley wall of rocks and stunted trees then travel almost on the level before hiking above a small, open basin. Mummy Mountain is the large cliff face directly ahead to the north. Curve left, enter woods and begin climbing to the end of a grassy swale then walk through it to the slope above Lawn Lake. Although the shore is treeless and grassy in places, the smooth, green surface of the lake actually suggested the name to some fishermen who were visiting the site in the early 1870's. The dam across the outlet was built in 1911.

To reach Crystal Lake continue along the trail that climbs above the northeast side of Lawn Lake. Pass an outbuilding on your left near the end of the climb and descend to lake level. Resume climbing and wind up the open slope to the junction of the trail to Rowe Glacier at 7.1 miles. Keep left and after a short climb and drop resume a steady uphill grade. Cross a few small creeks and continue up through a little valley of boulders, slabs and grass where marmots are plentiful. Pass a large tarn nestled among the boulders then go by a second one before coming to Crystal Lake.

Lawn Lake

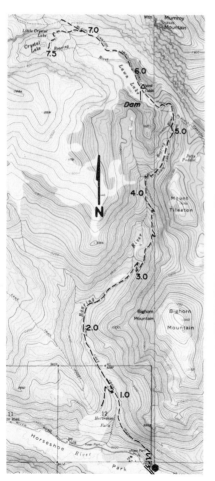

37 GEM LAKE

One day trip
Distance: 2 miles one way
Elevation gain: 1,110 feet
Allow 1½ hours one way
Usually open June through September
High point: 8,830 feet
Topographic map:
   U.S.G.S. Estes Park, Colo.
   7.5′   1961

The climb to Gem Lake is the most easterly hike in Rocky Mountain National Park and the terrain and vegetation along the trip are much different than that only a few miles to the west on higher and less arid slopes. Particularly interesting are the smooth, rounded rock formations that comprise Lumpy Ridge on whose crest Gem Lake is tucked. Near the end of the hike you will have a panoramic view of the portion of the Continental Divide within the central region of the Park and an aerial-like view of the city of Estes Park. Although the trip is short, the trail grade is moderately steep for much of its distance. Carry drinking water as the single source along the route may not be dependable.

Just east of the center of Estes Park turn north on MacGregor Avenue at the sign pointing to Devils Gulch and Glen Haven. Keep straight at the next intersection then after three-quarters mile curve right, stay-ing on the main road. Three-quarters mile farther be watching for a parking area off the road on your left (north). A sign stating Horse Trail — Gem Lake identifies the beginning of the hike.

Walk on the level road through private property for 0.2 mile before beginning to travel on a wide trail. As you start to climb enter woods and pass near the first of the many wierd rock formations you will enjoy along the route. Continue up an erratic and sometimes steep grade and at 0.7 mile enter Rocky Mountain National Park. A short distance from the boundary switchback up to your right. A path to the left at the turn leads to a small spring. Continue up and as you gain elevation you will have views of Lake Estes, Longs Peak and the area around Bear Lake.

Drop slightly then travel at a moderate uphill grade into a narrow canyon filled with aspen, conifers and varied rock groupings. Where the trail comes to a flat area and turns right, look left for a large, isolated rock with a hole through its upper end. The trail descends a few feet then resumes winding up through the canyon to the top of the ridge. Just before reaching the lake you will have a good view down onto Estes Park. In 1859 Joel Estes and one of his sons were the first white men to see then settle in the valley or "park" that today bears his name. Unlike most of the lakes in the Park, Gem Lake does not lie in a cirque but instead occupies a pocket on a ridge top surrounded by massive boulders. The lake has no inlet or outlet, the water level being maintained by seepage, rainfall and evaporation.

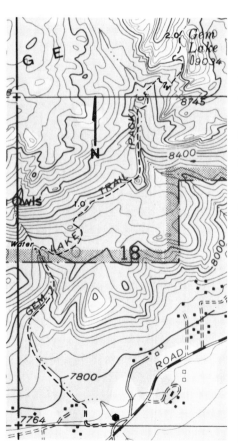

Trail below Gem Lake

38 DEER MOUNTAIN

One day trip
Distance: 1.6 miles one way
Elevation gain: 1,100 feet
Allow 1½ hours one way
Usually open June through September
High point: 10,000 feet
Topographic map:
    U.S.G.S. Estes Park, Colo.
    7.5′   1961

Deer Mountain is the high point of the ridge that separates the Beaver Meadows and Fall River Entrances to Rocky Mountain National Park. Visitors to Horseshoe Park below the northwest end of Deer Ridge have an especially good view of the cluster of massive boulders comprising the summit of the mountain. However, the trail passes to the south of the rocky crest so you will need to climb cross-country for about 100 yards to reach the viewpoint.

Carry water as none is available along the hike. Although not especially high or exposed, the ridge frequently is struck by lightning during electrical storms.

The hike begins on the north side of the road about 100 yards east of the Deer Ridge Junction on Trail Ridge Road. This junction is 2.8 miles west of the Beaver Meadows Entrance to Rocky Mountain National Park and 2.4 miles west and south of the Fall River Entrance. Parking spaces are available along the shoulders of the highway. The actual trailhead is identified by a large sign stating Horse Trail — Deer Mountain.

Drop slightly for 100 yards to the junction of the North Deer Mountain Trail to Estes Park. Keep right and climb gradually through the park-like setting of widely-spaced trees. Descend for a short distance then begin a gradual uphill traverse along the grassy, aspen-dotted slope. Along this stretch you will have views down onto Moraine Park and across to Longs Peak and the area around Bear Lake. Switchback to the left and soon enter coniferous woods.

Begin a series of short, moderately-graded switchbacks. Eventually, you will be able to see down onto Horseshoe Park. Make a long traverse on the northwest slope of Deer Mountain and at 1.0 mile resume switchbacking. A short distance beyond the last switchback and where the trail begins traversing in an easterly direction at a gradual grade, turn left, leaving the established route. Climb cross-country for 100 yards to the rock outcroppings on the crest. From this perch you can enjoy views of the Mummy Range including Ypsilon Mountain to the northwest, Twin Sisters Peaks and the Many Parks Curve area of Trail Ridge Road. The main trail continues at an almost level grade along the broad central portion of the crest then descends toward Estes Park.

Moraine Park and Longs Peak

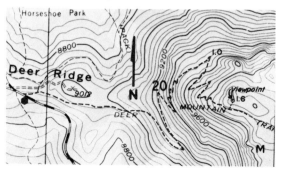

39 CUB LAKE AND MILL CREEK BASIN

One day trip or backpack
Distance: 4.2 miles one way
Elevation gain: 1,270 feet, loss 430 feet
Allow 3 to 3½ hours one way
Usually open late June through September
High point: 9,420 feet
Topographic map:
    U.S.G.S. McHenrys Peak, Colo.
    7.5'   **1957**

Since spectacular alpine scenery is plentiful in Rocky Mountain National Park, the gentle setting of Mill Creek Basin is enjoyed as much for the pleasing contrast it affords as for its own beauty. The Basin is an aspen-splashed meadow surrounded by low wooded slopes and the landscape is especially attractive when the aspen bear the yellow, gold and red leaves of fall. Mill Creek, and later the Basin, was named for the lumber mill that operated here in the late 1870's.

A strenuous and scenic loop trip can be made by combining this hike with No.'s 40 and 41. The loop is 15 miles long and involves 3,000 feet of elevation gain. If you decide to make the circuit, the preferable route is to visit Fern and Odessa Lakes first, climb to Lake Helene then descend along Bierstadt Moraine to Mill Creek Basin. (Refer to No. 40 for specific information.)

Proceed 0.1 mile west of the Beaver Meadows Entrance to Rocky Mountain National Park or 2.7 miles southeast of the Deer Ridge Junction of Trail Ridge Road (U.S. 34) to a sign pointing to Bear Lake and turn south. Drive downhill for one mile and turn right at the sign identifying the road to Moraine Park Campground and Fern Lake Trailhead. Proceed one-quarter mile and turn left 30 yards beyond a sign indicating the road to Cub and Fern Lakes Trailheads. The pavement ends after one mile near the parking area for a more easterly trail to Cub Lake and, although level, the dirt road is very narrow. After another

mile come to a parking area at the road's end. A sign at the west side of the turn-around marks the beginning of the Fern Lake Trail.

Walk along the wooded valley floor, generally at a level grade but with a few minor ups and downs. Occasionally, the trail travels close to the Big Thompson River and at 1.5 miles the route passes under the immense boulders of Arch Rocks. One-half mile farther come to a large bridge at The Pool. Just beyond the west side of the span is the junction of the trail to Fern Lake.

Keep left, go through woods for several yards to a side trail, turn left and pass a sign indicating the route to Cub Lake. Drop slightly for several feet then begin climbing moderately along the slope. The woods become quite dense along one stretch and the trail crosses two small streams. Briefly wind up through an open, rocky area then reenter woods and continue to the junction of the side trail to Cub Lake. To visit it, turn left and go through woods for one-third mile to a point above the shore. The west end of the lake usually is covered with lily pads.

To continue the hike to Mill Creek Basin turn right at the junction and wind up at a steeper grade through coniferous woods sprinkled with aspen. At 3.0 miles begin traversing up the densely forested slope where you will have glimpses down onto Cub Lake. As you near the top of the ridge the vegetation becomes less lush and at the crest there is no ground cover between the widely-spaced pine trees. Descend, and after 0.5 mile begin traveling above the northwestern edge of the meadows of Mill Creek Basin. Come to the junction of a trail to Hallowell Park and keep right along an open slope. After several hundred feet pass an immense fireplace on your left and an outbuilding. The route continues around the edge of the meadow to the crossing of Mill Creek then comes to a junction where one trail goes east to Hallowell Park and the other heads southwest to Bierstadt and Bear Lakes.

Fall color in Mill Creek Basin

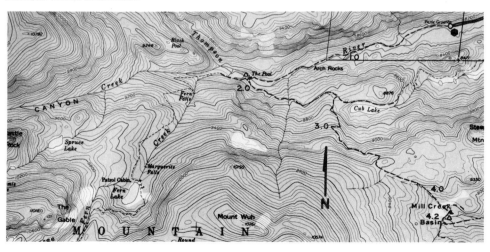

40 FERN AND ODESSA LAKES

One day trip or backpack
Distance: 5 miles one way
Elevation gain: 1,920 feet
Allow 3 to 3½ hours one way
Usually open late June through September
High point: 10,020 feet
Topographic map:
   U.S.G.S. McHenrys Peak, Colo.
   7.5'   **1957**

Like most hikes in the Park, the trail to Fern and Odessa Lakes travels through several different settings. For the first two miles the route parallels the Big Thompson River at the base of a steep rock wall then it climbs through deep woods to Fern Lake. The lodge near the east shore was built in 1910 (and later enlarged) and was operated until 1939. One mile farther you will reach Odessa Lake at the base of the Little Matterhorn. From the northeast it indeed does resemble a small version of the mountain that straddles the border between Italy and Switzerland.

If you have the time and energy you are urged to continue one mile beyond Odessa Lake along the steep wall of Joe Mills Mountain to Lake Helene (No. 41). A strenuous loop trip down Bierstadt Moraine to Mill Creek Basin that would add eight miles and 1,200 feet of elevation gain also is possible.

Drive 0.1 mile west of the Beaver Meadows Entrance to Rocky Mountain National Park or 2.7 miles southeast from the Deer Ridge Junction of Trail Ridge Road (U.S. 34) to a sign pointing to Bear Lake and turn south. Proceed downhill for one mile and turn right at the sign identifying the road to Moraine Park Campground and Fern Lake Trailhead. Travel one-quarter mile and turn left 30 yards beyond a sign identifying the road to Cub and Fern Lakes Trailheads. The pavement ends after one mile and, although level, the dirt road is very narrow. After another mile come to a parking area at the road's end. A sign at the west side of the turnaround marks the beginning of the Fern Lake Trail.

Walk along the nearly level valley floor. At 1.5 miles the route passes under the immense boulders of Arch Rocks and one-half mile farther comes to a large bridge at The Pool. Just beyond the west side of the span meet the junction of the trail to Cub Lake (No. 39).

Keep right and several yards farther keep right again. Climb a short distance then walk at a nearly level grade through woods. Pass a sign indicating campsites to the right and soon resume climbing. Cross Fern Creek on a bridge and wind loosely through woods then turn sharply left and traverse up a slope to Fern Falls. Switchback to the right and continue climbing through woods for 1.4 miles to the junction of the unimproved trail to Spruce Lake. Keep straight, climb 150 feet to the low ridge above Fern Lake and turn left.

Descend to the bridge across the outlet creek and walk along the shore past the former lodge. Travel through the edge of a large boulder field then reenter woods and begin climbing at a steady, moderate grade. At 4.9 miles come to a fork in the trail and keep right as indicated by the sign. Travel beside Fern Creek through a small canyon, cross a foot bridge and several yards farther come to Odessa Lake.

To make the recommended side trip to Lake Helene, keep left at the fork at 4.9 miles and climb at a steady, moderate grade along the valley wall, soon leaving the timber. Near the crest at the head of the spectacular rocky gorge where the trail curves to the east be watching for a spur on your right to Lake Helene. To do the Mill Creek Basin loop trip, take the main trail east from Lake Helene as described in the text for No. 41 and at the junction of the trail to Bear Lake at 0.4 mile follow the route to Bierstadt Lake. Soon begin descending and keep left at two junctions, following the signs pointing to Mill Creek. Turn left at the junction near the south edge of Mill Creek Basin and complete the circuit as described in the text for No. 39.

The Little Matterhorn

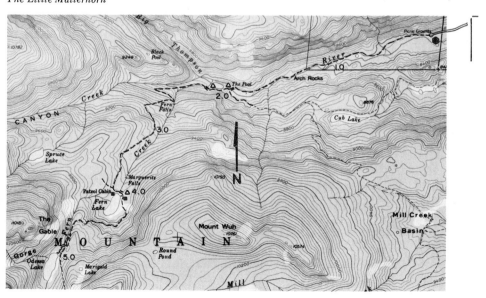

41 LAKE HELENE

One day trip
Distance: 3.5 miles one way
Elevation gain: 1,440 feet
Allow 2 hours one way
Usually open late June though September
High point: 10,690 feet
Topographic map:
    U.S.G.S. McHenrys Peak, Colo.
    7.5'   1957

Flattop Mountain

Lake Helene lies in a picturesque basin directly below Flattop Mountain at the head of a spectacular rocky gorge. Small glaciers cling to the walls of the several cirques above the lake to the northwest between Flattop and Notchtop Mountains. You are urged to extend the hike by following the moderately graded trail that traverses down the precipitous eastern wall of the gorge for one mile to Odessa Lake at the base of Little Matterhorn (see No. 40).

Proceed 0.1 mile west of the Beaver Meadows Entrance to Rocky Mountain National Park or 2.7 miles southeast from the Deer Ridge Junction of Trail Ridge Road (U.S. 34) to a sign pointing to Bear Lake and turn south. Drive downhill for one mile and keep straight where side roads go right to Moraine Park Campground and left to the Visitor Center. Continue eight miles to the end of the road at the Bear Lake Parking Area. Follow a sign at the east end of the turnaround indicating 100 feet to Bear Lake.

Where you come near the shore keep right and continue 50 feet along the paved path that circles the lake to a sign on your right stating Flattop Trail. Turn right and wind up through an attractive aspen grove to the junction of the trail to Bierstadt Lake. Turn left and traverse up the slope that affords a view down onto Bear Lake and across to Longs Peak during an open stretch. Cross to the opposite side of the ridge and walk on the level above a cluster of boulders before climbing a short distance in woods to the junction of the trail to Flattop Mountain (No. 43).

Keep right and climb moderately through woods then traverse above the head of Bierstadt Moraine that stretches out to the northeast. As you gain elevation you will be able to see Bierstadt Lake near the eastern end of the flat crest. At the edge of a grassy, open area come to a stream and an inviting snack stop. Continue up at an easy grade just at the edge of timberline. Briefly hike in deeper woods before traversing a scree slope then resume traveling through conifers to a sign identifying dry Mill Creek.

Wind up a slope of boulders, grass and trees then travel along a wooded slope, passing a sign identifying Two Rivers Lake below. Walk on the level for a short distance then drop very gradually for 0.1 mile to a sign marking the side path to Lake Helene, a portion of which you can see from the junction. Keep left and descend about 100 yards to the brushy north shore.

To make the recommended trip along the steep western wall of Joe Mills Mountain, named for Enos Mills' brother, to Lake Odessa, keep right on the main trail and after a short distance curve north into the rocky gorge.

94

Notchtop Mountain

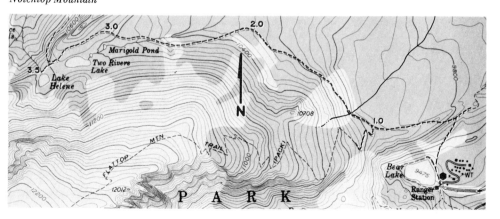

42 BIERSTADT LAKE

One day trip
Distance: 1.3 miles one way
Elevation gain: 600 feet
Allow ¾ to 1 hour one way
Usually open June through September
High point: 9,440 feet
Topographic maps:
    U.S.G.S. Longs Peak, Colo.
    7.5'   1961
    U.S.G.S. McHenrys Peak, Colo.
    7.5'   1957

Bierstadt Lake was named for Albert Bierstadt, a noted American artist who painted in the area in the 1870's. The lake rests on the top of massive Bierstadt Moraine. Along the first half of this short trail, aspen trees frame excellent views of the rugged back range.

The glaciers that deposited the debris comprising Bierstadt and the other moraines in the Park and carved the cirques and U-shaped valleys were, geologically speaking, recent performers in the pageant of forces that created the landforms seen today. At the time when the simplest life forms were beginning on earth the great sea that covered this region of the present day Rockies was beginning to recede and mountains slowly were rising. Eventually, the first mountains were worn away to a rolling plain and near the end of the Age of Reptiles about 60 million years ago the Rocky Mountains of today began rising. One million years ago the Ice Age began and glaciers formed in the high mountains. (The glaciers in the Colorado Rockies were not part of the massive fields of ice that covered much of North America during this period.) These glaciers receded, leaving behind the cirques, lakes, tarns, moraines and U-shaped valleys seen today. Only a few small glacial remnants remain in the Park and Trail No's. 43 and 46 visit two of them.

Drive 0.1 mile west of the Beaver Meadows Entrance to Rocky Mountain National Park or 2.7 miles southeast from the Deer Ridge Junction of Trail Ridge Road (U.S. 34) to a sign pointing to Bear Lake and turn south. Proceed downhill for one mile and keep straight where side roads go right to Moraine Park Campground and left to the Visitor Center. Continue five miles to a sign identifying the parking area for the Bierstadt Lake Trail on the right (north) side of the road. The trail begins at the northwest edge of the parking area.

Climb for a few yards and just beyond the register curve right and continue through deep evergreen woods at a moderate, steady grade. As the trail begins switchbacking the conifers are replaced by aspen. Climb through an open area that affords especially good views then resume switchbacking up through deciduous woods and occasional clearings.

Pine and spruce resume their dominance at the crest of the moraine and the trail descends very gradually for a short distance. The grade soon becomes level and during one stretch the trail is along a dirt dike. Just beyond this built-up section come to the junction of the trail to Bear Lake. Keep right, walk along another dike and come to a second junction. Turn right and descend slightly. At a sign pointing to Bear Lake keep straight (right) and a short distance farther keep right again at an unsigned fork to the shore of Bierstadt Lake.

Hallett Peak from the Bierstadt Lake Trail

43 FLATTOP MOUNTAIN

One day trip
Distance: 4.5 miles one way
Elevation gain: 3,075 feet
Allow 3 to 3½ hours one way
Usually open July through September
High point: 12,324 feet
Topographic map:
    U.S.G.S. McHenrys Peak, Colo.
    7.5′   **1957**

The trail to the broad, level summit of Flattop Mountain climbs at a steady, moderate grade past a succession of scenic attractions. The final 1.5 miles are above timberline and during this portion you will have views to the east over Bierstadt Moraine and beyond to Estes Park and northwest to the highest sections of Trail Ridge Road. From the summit you can continue south a few hundred yards and have lunch at the edge of Tyndall Glacier, just below the crest. Hikers wanting a more strenuous trip can continue along the gentle western side of the Continental Divide and climb Hallett Peak or visit Andrews Glacier.

Proceed 0.1 mile west of the Beaver Meadows Entrance to Rocky Mountain National Park or 2.7 miles southeast from the Deer Ridge Junction of Trail Ridge Road (U.S. 34) to a sign pointing to Bear Lake and turn south. Drive downhill for one mile and keep straight where side roads go right to Moraine Park Campground and left to the Visitor Center. Continue eight miles to the end of the road at the Bear Lake Parking Area. Follow a sign at the east end of the turnaround stating Bear Lake 100 feet.

Where you come near the shore keep right and continue 50 feet along the paved path that circles the lake to a sign on your right identifying the Flattop Trail. Turn right and wind up through an attractive aspen grove to the junction of the trail to Bierstadt Lake. Turn left and traverse up the slope that affords a view down onto Bear Lake and across to Longs Peak during an open stretch. Cross to the opposite side of the ridge and walk on the level above a swale of boulders before climbing a short distance in woods to the junction of the trail to Lake Helene (No. 41). Turn left and begin a series of switchbacks through coniferous woods to the viewpoint above Dream Lake (see No. 44). Mills Lake sprawls on a bench across the valleys to the south (refer to No. 48).

Continue up through woods and at 2.7 miles come to timberline. About 100 yards from where the trees are replaced by brush and gnarled, stunted conifers be watching for a pipe on your right a few feet off the trail. This is the only source of drinking water along the hike. A short distance beyond the water pipe begin a series of switchbacks and at 3.0 miles pass the viewpoint 1,200 feet above Emerald Lake (No. 44). As you look to the south you can see that the rock mass often identified as Hallett Peak from Bear Lake is really the lower part of a ridge that, after rising another 700 feet, ends in its actual, and much less imposing, summit.

From the viewpoint continue climbing along the mountain side, where conies are plentiful. Curve to the less steep northeast slope and traverse at a gradual grade for about one mile. Pass a metal hitching post and continue the final few hundred yards to the flat summit area.

To reach Hallett Peak continue along the almost level trail and keep left at an unmarked fork. Walk south around the Tyndall Glacier cirque and make the easy climb to the summit from the west. To reach the viewpoint above Andrews Glacier and Tarn (No. 46) continue south along the crest past the head of Chaos Canyon and Otis Peak for one and three-quarter miles to Andrews Pass.

Longs Peak from the Flattop Mountain Trail

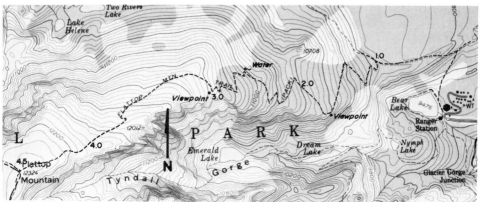

44 EMERALD LAKE

One day trip
Distance: 2 miles one way
Elevation gain: 650 feet
Allow 1 to 1½ hours one way
Usually open late June through September
High point: 10,100 feet
Topographic map:
   U.S.G.S. McHenrys Peak, Colo.
   7.5'   1957

The trail to Emerald Lake passes little Nymph Lake, profusely covered with lily pads, and long, narrow Dream Lake as it penetrates Tyndall Gorge, situated between the eastern ridges of Hallett Peak and Flattop Mountain. The few short stretches where the path is obscure during the final one-half mile adds a little challenge to this attractive and easy hike.

Drive 0.1 mile west of the Beaver Meadows Entrance to Rocky Mountain National Park or 2.7 miles southeast from the Deer Ridge Junction of Trail Ridge Road (U.S. 34) to a sign pointing to Bear Lake and turn south. Proceed downhill for one mile and keep straight where side roads go right to Moraine Park Campground and left to the Visitor Center. Continue eight miles to the end of the road at the Bear Lake Parking Area.

Follow a sign at the east end of the turnaround stating Bear Lake 100 feet. Where you come near the shore turn left at the sign pointing to Emerald Lake Trail. Keep straight for a few hundred feet, passing the ranger station on your right, to the junction of the trail to Glacier Gorge Junction and keep right, following the arrows pointing to Nymph, Dream and Emerald Lakes. The trail is paved for the first one-half mile and climbs very moderately through woods. Come to Nymph Lake and walk around its

east and north sides. Climb more noticeably, turn left and traverse 150 feet above the lake. Curve to the west along the face of an open slope and travel up among boulders and small aspens above a rugged little declivity. Just before a stream at 1.0 mile take the trail up to the right and meet the junction at a bridge of the trail to Lake Haiyaha (No. 45).

Keep right and after 0.1 mile come near the east end of Dream Lake. Walk parallel to the lake on the main trail and eventually travel close to the water's edge. At the west end of the lake follow the path to the right and after a few yards scramble for several feet up along a low rock band. Wind up, and sometimes down, through deep woods. Cross a little stream and scramble up rocks for a few feet. As you near the exit creek from Emerald Lake veer right through a tight little thicket of evergreens. Keep right where the trail appears to curve left around a large boulder and walk away from the stream across a small open bench. Traverse up a low rock band and again travel on a well-defined trail then squeeze between two huge boulders at the east end of Emerald Lake. The sheer rock face rising above the west end of the lake is not actually Hallett Peak but rather the east end of the ridge that continues up for 700 feet to the true summit.

Hallett Peak from Bear Lake

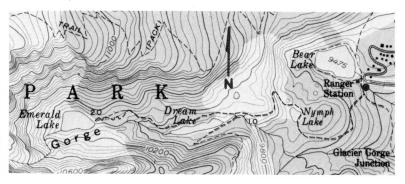

45 LAKE HAIYAHA

One day trip
Distance: 2.3 miles one way
Elevation gain: 810 feet, loss 100 feet
Allow 1 to 1½ hours one way
Usually open late June through September
High point: 10,240 feet
Topographic map:
  U.S.G.S. McHenrys Peak, Colo.
  7.5'   1957

Haiyaha is an Indian word for rock and the name was appropriately applied to Lake Haiyaha as the shores are surrounded by massive boulders. The hike to the lake can be done as a scenic loop if you want a slightly more strenuous trip. This circuit would add 1.8 miles and gain 300 feet.

Proceed 0.1 mile west of the Beaver Meadows Entrance to Rocky Mountain National Park or 2.7 miles southeast from the Deer Ridge Junction of Trail Ridge Road (U.S. 34) to a sign pointing to Bear Lake and turn south. Drive downhill for one mile and keep straight where side roads go right to Moraine Park Campground and left to the Visitor Center. Continue eight miles to the end of the road at the Bear Lake Parking Area.

Follow a sign at the east end of the turnaround indicating 100 feet to Bear Lake. Where you come near the shore turn left at the sign pointing to Emerald Lake Trail.

Keep straight for a few hundred feet, passing the ranger station on your right, to the junction of the trail to Glacier Gorge Junction. (If you make the recommended loop you will be returning along this trail.) Keep right, following the arrows pointing to Nymph, Dream and Emerald Lakes. The trail is paved for the first one-half mile and climbs very moderately through woods. Come to Nymph Lake and walk along its east and north sides. Climb more noticeably, turn left and traverse 150 feet above the lake. Curve to the west along the face of an open slope and hike above a rugged little declivity among boulders and small aspens. At 1.0 mile, just before a stream, take the trail up to the right and come to the junction of the trail to Dream and Emerald Lakes (No. 44) at a bridge.

Keep left and cross the span. Bear left where the trail forks after a few yards and a short distance farther pass an outbuilding on your left. Curve right and begin traversing up the densely wooded slope above Dream Lake. After climbing for 0.2 mile switchback to the left and continue up through woods. Curve right around the steep face of the ridge. Since the trees are sparse along this stretch, you can see down onto several lakes, including Bear and Nymph, and across to Longs Peak. Hike along the southeast side of the ridge and soon begin a gradual descent.

Cross the outlet from Lake Haiyaha on a footbridge then ford a smaller stream. Travel on the level for a short distance to the junction of the trail to Loch Vale. Keep right and climb very moderately, passing a tarn on your left and crossing a short stretch of boulders before coming to the rocky shore of the lake.

To make the recommended loop, keep left at the junction to Loch Vale and begin descending. The trail eventually levels off and 1.5 miles from the fork come to the four-way junction of the trails to Mills Lake (No. 48), Loch Vale (No. 47) and Glacier Gorge Junction. Take the far left trail and after a short climb and a traverse wind down to the large mileage sign just above the Glacier Gorge Junction Parking Area. (Refer to No. 47 for a detailed description of this section.) Keep straight, following the arrow pointing to Bear Lake, and climb for one-third mile to your starting point.

Gnarled tree at Lake Haiyaha

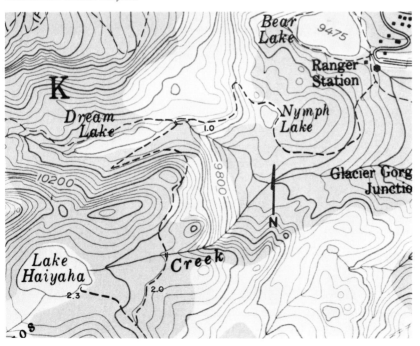

46 ANDREWS TARN

One day trip or backpack
Distance: 4.6 miles one way
Elevation gain: 2,180 feet
Allow 3 to 3½ hours one way
Usually open July through September
High point: 11,380 feet
Topographic map:
    U.S.G.S. McHenrys Peak, Colo.
    7.5'   1957

Aspen at Glacier Gorge

Tucked into niches on the east side of the peaks in Rocky Mountain National Park are five small remnants of the much larger glaciers that once crept down the slopes. Collecting melt water from Andrews Glacier, the second most southerly of the five, is a small lake of the same name perched on the edge of an only slightly larger bench. It is reached by a path that travels along the rocky floor of a spire-rimmed valley then winds steeply up to the tarn.

A side trip to Glass Lake and a view over Loch Vale would add only one mile and 250 feet of elevation gain. (Refer to No. 47.)

Drive 0.1 mile west of the Beaver Meadows Entrance to Rocky Mountain National Park or 2.7 miles southeast from the Deer Ridge Junction of Trail Ridge Road (U.S. 34) to a sign pointing to Bear Lake and turn south. Proceed downhill for one mile and keep straight where side roads go right to Moraine Park Campground and left to the Visitor Center. Continue 7.5 miles to the Glacier Gorge Parking Area. The trailhead is south across the road just above the steep curve of the highway and is marked by a large sign.

Turn left at the sign, cross a bridge and soon come to the junction of a spur to the Storm Pass Trail. Keep right and climb quite moderately, first crossing a small bridge then a larger one. Pass Alberta Falls at 0.5 mile and wind up to the junction of the North Longs Peak Trail (No. 49).

Keep right and continue climbing for a short distance then begin contouring above a canyon. Descend for several yards and come to the four-way junction of the trails to Black Lake (No. 48) and Haiyaha and Bear Lakes (No. 45). Take the middle of the three routes and traverse up at a moderate grade, soon entering the little gorge formed by Icy Brook. Climb in two complete sets of switchbacks then make a sweeping curve and come to the northeast end of The Loch. Turn right and enter a small open area where several side paths branch from the main route. Keep left at the first fork then, just before an outbuilding, bear right and a few feet farther stay left. Travel around the north shore of The Loch in a series of small ups and downs then begin climbing through woods. At 3.5 miles come to the junction of the trail to Glass Lake and Sky Pond, turn right and hop across a small stream.

Wind steeply up through woods for a few hundred yards then climb more moderately. Enter a valley and where a trail joins from your right near a meadow note the location of the junction so you will not miss it on the return. Hike along the southern slope of the valley and soon leave the deep timber. Traverse an area of small boulder fields, following circles of orange spray paint on the rocks, then just after crossing a small stream take the trail that climbs to the left. Follow the path along the floor of the rubble-strewn valley, keeping the stream on your left. At the base of the large rock mass in the center of the basin near the head of the valley cross the stream and wind up the gully to the south of the rocks. After climbing steeply for 0.2 mile come to Andrews Tarn at the edge of a small bench.

The Sharkstooth

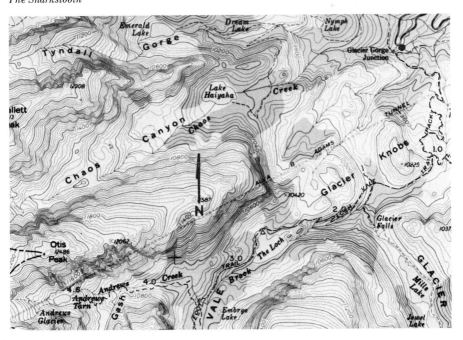

47 SKY POND

One day trip or backpack
Distance: 4.5 miles one way
Elevation gain: 1,700 feet
Allow 2½ to 3 hours one way
Usually open July through September
High point: 10,800 feet
Topographic map:
    U.S.G.S. McHenrys Peak, Colo.
    7.5′   1957

Loch Vale, the valley through which the trail travels for the last two miles of the hike, was named for a Mr. Locke but the spelling was changed to Loch, the Scottish work for lake. The final one-third mile from Glass Lake (also more pleasingly called Lake of Glass) to Sky Pond is along a level but very rocky cross-country route. However, for those who do not enjoy boulder hopping, Glass Lake affords a good stopping place with a fine view. Since the short, but steep, path to Andrews Tarn (No. 46) leaves the main route at 3.5 miles, you easily could combine the two hikes. This side trip would add a total of two miles and 1,000 feet of elevation gain.

Proceed 0.1 mile west of the Beaver Meadows Entrance to Rocky Mountain National Park or 2.7 miles southeast from the Deer Ridge Junction of Trail Ridge Road (U.S. 34) to a sign pointing to Bear Lake and turn south. Drive downhill for one mile and keep straight where side roads go right to Moraine Park Campground and left to the Visitor Center. Continue 7.5 miles to the Glacier Gorge Parking Area. The trailhead is south across the road just above the steep curve of the highway and is marked by a large sign.

Turn left at the sign and cross a bridge. Pass a beaver pond on your left and at the register come to the junction of a spur to the Storm Pass Trail. Keep right and climb moderately, soon crossing a small bridge then a larger one. Continue rising beneath conifers and aspen and pass Alberta Falls at 0.5 mile. Wind up, sometimes traveling close to the narrow, deep rocky gorge formed by Glacier Creek, to the junction of the North Longs Peak Trail (No. 49).

Keep right and continue climbing for a short distance then begin contouring around the most easterly of the two Glacier Knobs. Descend for several yards and come to the four-way junction of the trails to Black Lake (No. 48) and Haiyaha and Bear Lakes (No. 45). Take the middle of the three routes and traverse up at a moderate grade, soon entering the little gorge formed by Icy Brook. Climb in two complete sets of switchbacks then make a sweeping curve and come to the northeast end of The Loch. Turn right and enter a small open area where several side paths branch from the main route. Keep left at the first fork then, just before an outbuilding, bear right and a few feet farther stay left. Travel around the north shore of The Loch in a series of small ups and downs then begin climbing through woods. Pass under a huge overhanging rock face at the edge of Icy Brook and 0.1 mile farther come to the junction of the trail to Andrews Tarn.

Keep left, drop a few feet and hop across a small stream. Hike through woods and small clearings to the base of a rock scarp. Wind up the steep slope then scramble up the rock gulley beside Timberline Falls. During the climb you will be able to see back down to The Loch. Simultaneously, come to the edge of the basin, timberline and Glass Lake. To complete the hike travel near the northwest shore of Glass Lake then continue scrambling over small escarpments and large boulders to the barren north end of Sky Pond.

Timberline Falls

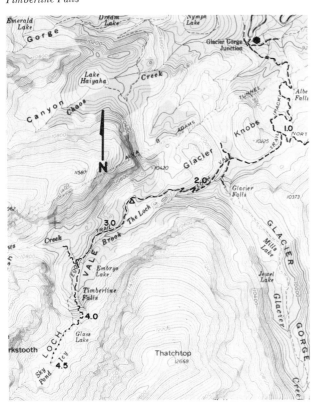

48 BLACK LAKE

One day trip or backpack
Distance: 5 miles one way
Elevation gain: 1,400 feet
Allow 3½ to 4 hours one way
Usually open July through September
High point: 10,620 feet
Topographic map:
   U.S.G.S. McHenrys Peak, Colo.
   7.5'   1957

The east side of the Continental Divide be-tween Flattop Mountain and Longs Peak was a region of heavy glaciation and the exceptionally scenic results are visited by a network of five trails (See No's. 44 through 48). Black Lake is the most southerly desti-nation in this group and lies beneath the almost vertical walls of McHenrys Peak at the head of three mile long Glacier Gorge.

Although not difficult to negotiate, the route beyond 2.0 miles is more of a path than a trail. Backpackers and hikers want-ing a more strenuous trip can climb for three-quarters mile above Black Lake, gain-ing about 1,000 feet of elevation, to the superb setting of Frozen Lake.

Drive 0.1 mile west of the Beaver Meadows Entrance to Rocky Mountain Na-tional Park or 2.7 miles southeast from the Deer Ridge Junction of Trail Ridge Road (U.S. 34) to a sign pointing to Bear Lake and turn south. Proceed downhill for one mile and keep straight where side roads go right to Moraine Park Campground and left to the Visitor Center. Continue 7.5 miles to the Glacier Gorge Parking Area. The trail-head is south across the road just above the steep curve of the highway and is marked by a large sign.

Turn left at the sign, cross a bridge and soon come to a junction of the spur to the Storm Pass Trail. Keep right and climb quite moderately, soon crossing a small bridge then a larger one. Pass Alberta Falls at 0.5 mile and wind up to the junction of the North Longs Peak Trail (No. 49).

Keep right and continue climbing for a short distance then travel on the level above a canyon. Wind down for several yards and come to the four-way junction of trails to Sky Pond (No. 47) and Andrews Tarn (No. 46) and to Haiyaha and Bear Lakes (No. 45). Keep left on the most easterly trail, pass an outbuilding on your left and soon drop slightly to the bridge over Icy Brook. Walk at a moderate grade then climb along a rocky slope for several yards to an area of slabs. Turn left as indicated by the cairns and after a short level stretch and descent cross Glacier Creek on a bridge. Turn right and climb for several hundred feet through a little aspen grove then walk over a level area of slabs and boulders to the end of Mills Lake.

The trail continues near the east shore of Mills Lake and where the route forks mid-way along its length you can follow either one. At the end of the lake come to a sign identifying Jewel Lake to the west. Beyond the small lake cross a marshy meadow on a log walkway then wind up through woods at an erratic grade with a few slight drops. Come to a small patch of boulders at the edge of a meadow. Cross the rocks and walk beside a wide stream for several yards then resume climbing along the slope.

Pass below a little waterfall at 4.2 miles and continue traversing through woods and meadows. Walk on the level through an open area then wind up a rock band beside Ribbon Falls. At the crest cross a small grassy area then some flat stones and come to the edge of Black Lake. Scramble over boulders along the northeast shore for sev-eral yards then walk through woods above the water before dropping to a clearing near an inlet creek.

To make the cross-country trip to Frozen Lake, climb beside the inlet creek near the campground and as the slope becomes more gradual curve southwest, pass under the face of the Spearhead and come to the lake's northeastern shore.

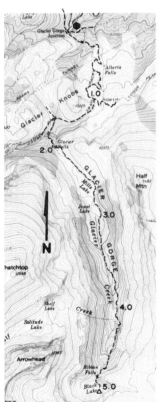

McHenrys Peak from Black Lake

49 NORTH LONGS PEAK TRAIL

One day trip or backpack
Distance: 8 miles one way to Boulder Field
Elevation gain: 4,400 feet
Allow 5 to 6 hours one way
Usually open July through September
High point: 13,500 feet
Topographic maps:
    U.S.G.S. Longs Peak, Colo.
    7.5'   1961
    U.S.G.S. McHenrys Peak, Colo.
    7.5'   1957

Indians, and later trappers, used Longs Peak, the highest in northern Colorado, and its neighbor Mt. Meeker as twin reference points when traveling on the plains. The natives called the peaks the Two Guides and the French trappers referred to them as The Two Ears. In 1820 Major Stephen Long led a party of 22 men along the Front Range. The map of his expedition showed Longs Peak as Highest Peak, but common usage soon affixed the Major's name to the mountain.

The established trail ends high above timberline at Boulder Field, a gently sloping expanse of huge rocks on the north shoulder of Longs Peak. Two short, but strenuous, side trips continue over boulders to spectacular viewpoints at the Keyhole and Chasm View, 1,700 feet directly above Chasm Lake. The weather can be especially inclement on Longs Peak so be prepared for wind and cold. Although many campsites are available at Boulder Field, the setting is austere.

Proceed 0.1 mile west of the Beaver Meadows Entrance to Rocky Mountain National Park or 2.7 miles southeast from the Deer Ridge Junction of Trail Ridge Road (U.S. 34) to a sign pointing to Bear Lake and turn south. Drive downhill for one mile and keep straight where side roads go right to Moraine Park Campground and left to the Visitor Center. Continue 7.5 miles to the Glacier Gorge Parking Area. The trailhead is south across the road just above the steep curve of the highway and is marked by a large sign.

Turn left at the sign and cross a bridge. Pass a beaver pond on your left and come to a junction of a spur to the Storm Pass Trail. Keep right and climb slightly, soon crossing a small bridge then a larger one. Continue rising beneath conifers and aspen and pass Alberta Falls. Wind up, sometimes traveling close to the narrow, deep rocky gorge formed by Glacier Creek, to the junction of the trail to Loch Vale (See No. 47) at 1.0 mile.

Keep left, drop slightly and cross the gorge on a sturdy bridge. The trail rises for a short distance then loses elevation to avoid a band of boulders. Traverse up a wooded slope and at the crest curve right and wind up through stunted timber to the edge of a large basin. Cross it, climbing moderately, and enter deeper timber as you approach the eastern wall. Curve left after crossing two streams and soon begin a series of long switchbacks. During this stretch you will see weathered remains of the huge Bear Lake Fire that devastated this area in the late 1800's.

Climb above timberline on the last switchback and pass between two knobby rock outcroppings, one above the trail and the other downslope. The trail makes a long, sweeping curve along the slope then travels on the level for a few hundred yards to Granite Pass and the junction of the trail to Chasm Lake (No. 53). Turn right and begin climbing in long, very gradual switchbacks. Come to a bench and walk on the level for a short distance to the north edge of Boulder Field. The trail stops at the rocks and the final several hundred yards to the end of the level stretch is easy boulder hopping.

To reach the Keyhole and the shelter just below it, bear right from the latrine at the south end of Boulder Field and scramble toward the notch on the skyline that has the outline of a keyhole, gaining 400 feet of elevation during the 0.5 mile of travel. The side trip to Chasm View is slightly more strenuous as it involves 0.7 mile and 500 feet of elevation gain. It is reached by bearing left at the latrine and climbing toward the flat place on the skyline just below where the slope to the summit steepens.

Stone shelter at the Keyhole

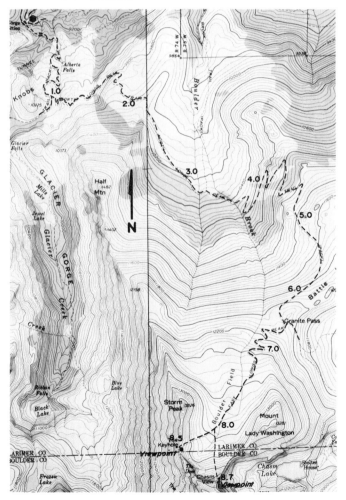

50 LILY MOUNTAIN

One day trip
Distance: 2 miles one way
Elevation gain: 1,256 feet, loss 260 feet
Allow 1½ hours one way
Usually open June through September
High point: 9,786 feet
Topographic map:
   U.S.G.S. Longs Peak, Colo.
    7.5′   1961

The flat, cozy high point on the ridge that forms Lily Mountain is a particularly inviting spot to relax. While resting on the crest you can see down onto the large complex of buildings comprising the Estes Park YMCA Camp and northeast over a farm-dotted valley to Lake Estes and Estes Park. Nearby are Twin Sisters Peaks and Longs Peak. The final few hundred feet to the summit is an easy and fun rock scramble. Carry water as none is available at the trailhead or along the hike.

Near the east end of Estes Park turn south from U.S. 34 onto U.S. 36. Go one-half mile then keep right on Colorado 7 and proceed 3.3 miles to the junction with Colorado 66. Keep left, continue on Colorado 7, and after nearly two miles drive through three rock cuts. About 50 yards south of the final one pass a sign on your right reading Lily Mountain Trail. Only a couple of parking spaces are available off the road near the sign. If you are approaching from the south on Colorado 7 travel 15 miles north from the junction of Colorado 7 and 72.

Traverse north along the partially wooded slope above the highway. The grade is erratic but never steep. After 0.4 mile of slight climbs and drops the trail makes several very short switchbacks then traverses to a large rock outcropping. After switchbacking a few more times resume traveling along the mountain side with minor ups and downs for 0.4 mile to an unmarked junction of a trail that descends toward the highway.

Keep left and climb several yards to a crest. Curve left and continue up near the edge of the ridge for a short distance then wind up through deeper woods in a generally southwesterly direction with the grade steepening about 0.5 mile from the junction. Drop slightly and pass some knobby rock outcroppings on your left. About 60 yards beyond them the trail becomes faint then stops. Turn right and climb a few yards then scramble left up the slope for 100 yards to the summit.

Twin Sisters Peaks from Lily Mountain

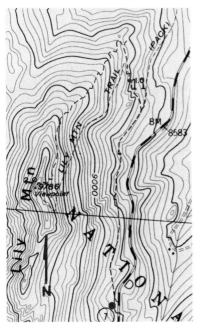

Sharkface Rock

51 EUGENIA MINE

One day trip
Distance: 1.5 miles one way
Elevation gain: 420 feet
Allow 1 hour one way
Usually open June through September
High point: 9,820 feet
Topographic map:
    U.S.G.S. Longs Peak, Colo.
    7.5′   **1961**

Mine relic

A large, dilapidated log cabin and some machinery near the tailings are the most obvious remains of the Eugenia Mine that was active during the first part of the 1900's. The hike is easy and short and you will want to allow extra time to explore the workings.

Turn south from U.S. 34 onto U.S. 36 near the east end of Estes Park. Proceed one-half mile then keep right on Colorado 7 and drive 3.3 miles to the junction with Colorado 66. Stay left, continuing on Colorado 7, and drive 5.2 miles to a large sign on your right marking the road to Longs Peak Campground. If you are approaching from the south, travel 12 miles north on Colorado 7 from the junction of Colorado 7 and 72. Turn west and drive along the dirt road that becomes paved at the Park boundary. One mile from the highway turn left at a fork as indicated by the sign pointing to Longs Peak Trail. Drive the short distance to the large parking area at the end of the road.

The trail begins just south of the ranger station and climbs at a moderate grade through woods of conifers and aspen. After 0.6 mile come to the junction of the trail to Chasm Lake (No. 53). Turn right and walk on the level through a grove of small aspen. However, soon only evergreens comprise the forest cover. Although the trail grade becomes erratic, the short stretches of climbing and descending are quite moderate and during one stretch the trail surface is rocky and rooty. Ford a shallow stream and immediately come to the remains of the log cabin that housed the miner's family. To reach the tailings, turn left and walk a few hundred feet. From here paths climb steeply up the slope to various digging sites.

Former living quarters at the mine

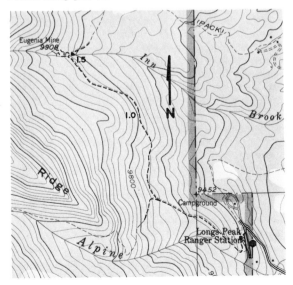

52 TWIN SISTERS PEAKS

One day trip
Distance: 3.5 miles one way
Elevation gain: 2,375 feet
Allow 2½ to 3 hours one way
Usually open June through September
High point: 11,413 feet
Topographic map:
   U.S.G.S. Longs Peak, Colo.
   7.5′   **1961**

Before the turn of the century, the peak was known as Lily Mountain from the western side and Twin Sisters from the eastern, probably because the rocky double summits appear as one when seen from certain angles. The view from the lookout on the most westerly (and lower) of the twin peaks extends north past Fort Collins, east over the plains, south to Mount Evans and beyond Longs Peak to near the northwestern boundary of Rocky Mountain National Park. The grade is moderate and steady for almost the entire distance and no water is available at the trailhead or along the hike.

Turn south from U.S. 34 onto U.S. 36 near the east end of Estes Park. Go one-half mile then keep right on Colorado 7 and drive 3.3 miles to the junction with Colorado 66. Keep left, continuing on Colorado 7, and proceed 4.2 miles to a large sign on your left stating Twin Sisters Trail. If you are approaching from the south, travel on Colorado 7 to a point 13 miles north of the junction of Highways 7 and 72. Turn east onto the dirt road and drive for 100 yards. A turnout for parking is just beyond where the road curves left.

Walk up the road 150 feet to where private drives go to the right and left. Take the trail in the middle and after a short, steep climb begin traversing up in woods at a moderate grade. Pass through a gate and continue along the forested slope. Near 1.0 mile begin a series of many switchbacks. Periodically, you will have glimpses of the Indian Peaks area to the southwest and the east face of Longs Peak. As the elevation increases, the trees become shorter, stouter and less dense and the forest floor is sprinkled with rocks.

Come to a saddle at 2.5 miles and curve right. Soon the trail becomes steeper and

The Lookout

rocky then it switchbacks a few times. Lake Estes and a portion of the plains are visible to the north and just at timberline you can see the lookout above to the southeast. Climb along a boulder field where conies make their homes, switchbacking a few times, to a stone shelter at the edge of a narrow saddle between the two summit peaks. Wind up the final few yards to the lookout tower. The Mummy Range, the route of Trail Ridge Road above timberline and Specimen Mountain are on the horizon to the northwest. The mountains beyond Bear Lake and, slightly closer, Wild Basin south of Longs Peak also can be studied.

116

East face of Longs Peak from Twin Sisters Lookout

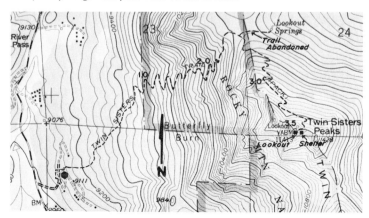

53 CHASM LAKE

One day trip or backpack
Distance: 5.5 miles one way
Elevation gain: 2,400 feet, loss 100 feet
Allow 3 to 3½ hours one way
Usually open July through September
High point: 11,800 feet
Topographic map:
   U.S.G.S. Longs Peak, Colo.
   7.5'   1961

Probably the best known feature in Rocky Mountain National Park is the sheer east face of Longs Peak. Chasm Lake lies in a cirque at the base of this 2,450 foot wall. Just one-quarter mile below the barren, majestic setting of the lake, a sturdy shelter cabin rests on a grassy little bench where marmots, ground squirrels and conies make their homes.

A side trip to Boulder Field at the 12,800 foot level on Longs Peak can be made by taking the trail from the junction at 4.0 miles and climbing along the northeastern slope of Mount Lady Washington to Granite Pass and the junction of the North Longs Peak Trail (No. 49). This climb would add a total of three miles and 1,300 feet of elevation gain.

Near the east end of Estes Park turn south from U.S. 34 onto U.S. 36. Proceed one-half mile then keep right on Colorado 7 and drive 3.3 miles to the junction with Colorado 66. Stay left, continuing on Colorado 7, and drive 5.2 miles to a large sign on your right marking the road to Longs Peak Campground. If you are approaching from the south, travel 12 miles north on Colorado 7 from the junction of Colorado 7 and 72. Turn west along the dirt road that becomes paved at the Park boundary. One mile from the highway turn left at a fork indicated by the sign pointing to Longs Peak Trail. A large parking area is at the road's end.

The trail begins just south of the ranger station and climbs at a moderate grade beneath a mixture of aspen and conifers. After 0.6 mile come to the junction of the short trail to Eugenia Mine (No. 51), keep left and soon begin switchbacking. Come near Alpine Brook and make one more switchback before traveling in a westerly direction for three-quarters mile. Curve left and come near Alpine Brook for a second time. Climb in a series of short switchbacks then finally cross Alpine Brook on a long foot bridge.

Leave the woods and climb in one long switchback along Mills Moraine to the junction near timberline of the path to Jims Grove. This moraine and a lake and glacier were named for Enos Mills, innkeeper, mountain guide and lecturer who was the individual most responsible for the creation of Rocky Mountain National Park. Turn left and continue gradually up the moraine. Keep on the main trail where you pass a faint path that goes uphill but a short distance farther turn right at the well-worn side path marked by a large cairn. Wind up the open slope at a very moderate grade, following the tall cairns. The thin band of the plains, Estes Cone and Twin Sisters Peaks become visible as you climb higher. At the crest come to a four-way junction. The trail to the right is the one you will follow if you make the side trip to Boulder Field. Granite Pass is on the crest of the ridge to the northwest.

Keep straight and drop a few feet, passing a sign indicating the way to Chasm Lake. After a short, moderate stretch of climbing begin a gradual downhill traverse along a steep canyon wall. Travel along the slope above Peacock Pond and Columbine Falls and come to the bench at the head of the valley. The final one-quarter mile to Chasm Lake follows the faint path up the gully behind the shelter. At the crest of the first pitch bear left across grass and rock then turn right and scramble up the final short distance to the rim above the lake.

Summit of Longs Peak from Chasm Lake

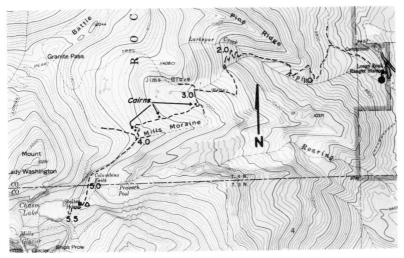

54 SANDBEACH LAKE

One day trip or backpack
Distance: 4 miles one way
Elevation gain: 1,965 feet
Allow 2½ hours one way
Usually open late June through September
High point: 10,295 feet
Topographic map:
    U.S.G.S. Allens Park, Colo.
    7.5′   1957

Wild Basin is located in the southeastern corner of Rocky Mountain National Park and the five main trails that penetrate the area are described in this guide. Hike No. 58 goes to Finch Lake, the most southerly trip in the Park, and Trail No's. 55, 56 and 57 travel up the large, wooded valley formed by North St. Vrain Creek to Lion, Thunder and Bluebird Lakes. The sandy beaches that suggested the name of Sandbeach Lake were inundated when a dam was constructed in the early 1900's.

Near the east end of Estes Park turn south from U.S. 34 onto U.S. 36. Drive one-half mile then keep right on Colorado 7 and proceed 11 miles to the community of Meeker Park. One and one-half miles farther pass a cluster of buildings where an obscure sign on the left (south) side of the road states Wild Basin Ranger Station. (The sign, which is easy to miss, is several yards northeast of the small bridge over North St. Vrain Creek.) If you are approaching from the south, drive 8.1 miles north on Colorado 7 from the junction of Colorado 7 and 72. Turn north onto the dirt road and drive past a few buildings. Where the main dirt road curves left and travels above the south shore of Copeland Lake, proceed straight to an ill-defined parking area beneath a grove of trees. The Sandbeach Lake sign identifies the trailhead.

Climb steeply along the wooded southern slope of Copeland Moraine. (The moraine, a falls, lake and mountain in Wild Basin are named for John B. Copeland who homesteaded 320 acres here in the late 1880's.) Where a trail contours to the left keep straight and continue uphill. After 0.2 mile curve west and hike at a much more moderate grade. Enter Rocky Mountain National Park at 0.6 mile and continue traversing above the valley. Make one short set of switchbacks, go over the crest to the other side of the ridge and come to the junction of the Meeker Park trail.

Keep straight (left) and travel uphill for a short distance. Walk on the level for about 0.2 mile then climb again to the crossing of Campers Creek. The trail turns left on the opposite side of the stream and traverses up to a ridge top. Turn right and walk along the crest then begin a series of minor ups and downs, passing through a grove of aspen and low bushes during one stretch. Continue up through woods and cross Hunters Creek at 3.1 miles. Climb moderately steeply then resume traveling at a more gentle grade. A short distance beyond a stretch where the trail has been built up above the surrounding terrain come to the northeast end of Sandbeach Lake. An outhouse is to the right off the trail.

First snow of autumn

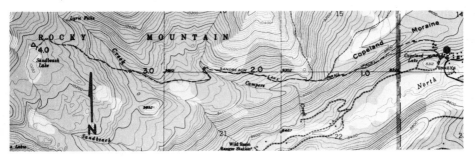

55 LION LAKE

One day trip or backpack
Distance: 8 miles one way
Elevation gain: 2,630 feet
Allow 3½ to 4 hours one way
Usually open July through September
High point: 11,130 feet
Topographic maps:
  U.S.G.S. Allens Park, Colo.
  7.5'   1957
  U.S.G.S. Isolation Peak, Colo.
  7.5'   1958

The hike to Lion Lake No. 1 is one of the most scenic trips in Wild Basin. Numerous rock outcroppings are separated by fields of grass and the tarns and clusters of conifers scattered over the terrain add to the already attractive landscape. The numerous benches above the lake invite exploration and if you are backpacking and have time, you are encouraged to take the trails to Thunder Lake (No. 56) and Bluebird Lake (No. 57).

Turn south from U.S. 34 onto U.S. 36 near the east end of Estes Park. Drive one-half mile then keep right on Colorado 7 and proceed 11 miles to Meeker Park. One and one-half miles farther pass a cluster of buildings where an obscure sign on the left (south) side of the road points to Wild Basin Ranger Station. (The sign, which is easy to miss, is several yards northeast of the small bridge over North St. Vrain Creek.) From the south, drive 8.1 miles north on Colorado 7 from the junction of Colorado 7 and 72. Turn north onto the dirt road and drive past a few buildings then curve left around the east and south shores of Copeland Lake. Continue for two miles to the road's end at a picnic area and the Wild Basin Ranger Station. The trail begins at the southwest side of the parking area near a large bulletin board at the entrance to the turnaround.

Immediately cross two large bridges then travel at a very moderate grade with a few short, gentle stretches of ups and downs. After 0.2 mile pass a sign on your left indicating the path to Copeland Falls and continue along the wooded slope. At 1.8 miles come to an elaborate bridge over North St. Vrain Creek. Climb more noticeably through deeper woods for one-third mile to

the junction of the spur to Finch Lake Trail at Calypso Cascades.

Curve right and cross the complex of streams on three bridges. Although the grade still is irregular, the trail begins climbing more consistently. Three-quarters mile beyond the Cascades pass an outbuilding to your left off the trail just before coming to a sign identifying Ouzel Falls. Cross the stream on a bridge and 200 yards farther come to a viewpoint over the valley and across to Longs Peak and Mt. Meeker. The trail drops to avoid a high rock band then resumes rising moderately to the junction of the trail to Bluebird Lake. Keep straight (right) and continue up at a moderate grade. Cross a bridge, curve sharply left at the crest above the span and follow the trail that parallels closest to the stream. Hike at a quite moderate grade then climb more noticeably to the junction of the trail to Thunder Lake.

Turn right and climb very steeply along the rocky trail for 100 yards. The grade then becomes more moderate and the surface smooth as the trail winds up around many boulders. Although generally uphill, the circuitous route also has a few level stretches. Climb to a flat ridge crest and walk on the level before going up over a hump. Descend into deep woods then climb steeply. After the grade moderates come to the end of a grassy swale where the trail becomes faint. Walk through the little valley and where you pass a tarn on your left turn and go around its western side. Drop gradually for several yards and come to the southern tip of Lion Lake No. 1. An explorative trip would be to climb cross-country to Lion Lake No. 2 and Snowbank Lake.

Chiefs Head Peak

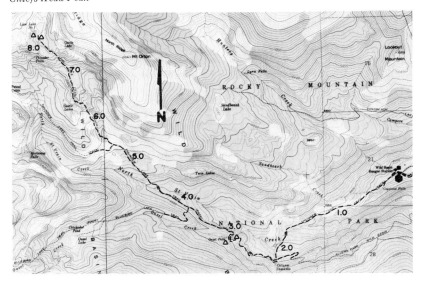

56 THUNDER LAKE

One day trip or backpack
Distance: 7.5 miles one way
Elevation gain: 2,170 feet
Allow 3 to 3½ hours one way
Usually open July through September
High point: 10,650 feet
Topographic maps:
    U.S.G.S. Allens Park, Colo.
    7.5'   1957
    U.S.G.S. Isolation Peak, Colo.
    7.5'   1958

All water in Wild Basin eventually drains into North St. Vrain Creek and the entire hike to Thunder Lake follows beside the stream or high along the slopes of the valley carved by the flow. In the late 1830's one of the St. Vrain brothers and a second man established a store near the present town of Gilcrest. The post, where Indians exchanged furs for items such as mirrors, eventually became known as Fort St. Vrain and the stream that flowed into the South Platte River 1.5 miles to the west of the store was called St. Vrain Creek.

If you are backpacking on this hike you can see more of the scenic terrain in the Basin by following the trails to Lion and Bluebird Lakes (No's. 55 and 57).

Near the east end of Estes Park turn south from U.S. 34 onto U.S. 36. Drive one-half mile then keep right on Colorado 7 and proceed 11 miles to Meeker Park. One and one-half miles farther pass a cluster of buildings where an obscure sign on the left (south) side of the road points to Wild Basin Ranger Station. (The sign, which is easy to miss, is several yards northeast of the small bridge over North St. Vrain Creek.) If you are approaching from the south, drive 8.1 miles north on Colorado 7 from the junction of Colorado 7 and 72. Turn north onto the dirt road and drive past a few buildings then curve left around the east and south shores of Copeland Lake. Continue for two miles to the road's end at a picnic area and the Wild Basin Ranger Station. The trail begins at the southwest side of the parking area near a large bulletin board you pass on your left as you enter the turnaround.

Immediately cross two large bridges then travel at a very moderate grade with a few short, gentle stretches of ups and downs. After 0.2 mile pass a sign on your left indicating the path to Copeland Falls and continue along the wooded slope. At 1.8 miles come to a bridge over North St. Vrain Creek then climb more noticeably through deeper woods for one-third mile to the junction of the spur to the Finch Lake Trail at Calypso Cascades.

Curve right and cross the complex of streams on three bridges. Although still irregular, the trail grade begins rising more consistently. Three-quarters mile beyond the Cascades pass an outbuilding to your left off the trail just before coming to Ouzel Falls. Cross the stream on a bridge and 200 yards farther come to a viewpoint over the valley and across to Longs Peak and Mt. Meeker. The trail drops to avoid a high rock band then resumes climbing moderately to the junction of the trail to Bluebird Lake. Keep straight (right) and continue up at a moderate grade. Cross a bridge, curve sharply left at the crest above the span and follow the trail that parallels closest to the stream. Hike at a quite moderate grade then climb more noticeably to the junction of the trail to Lion Lake.

Keep left and continue traversing along the slope. Switchback once and pass through an area of stunted trees and rocky terrain. Enter deeper woods and soon have glimpses into the Eagle Basin area high on the slopes across the deep valley. Cross a good-sized stream and continue climbing at a very moderate grade, passing a small meadow on your left at one point. Cross a smaller brook and at the end of one final uphill stretch come to a sign stating Thunder Lake. The trail curves left and winds down to the grassy area at the east end of the lake. An outbuilding is located to the right of the trail just before the clearing. A well-defined trail continues past the patrol cabin and along the north shore.

Thunder Lake

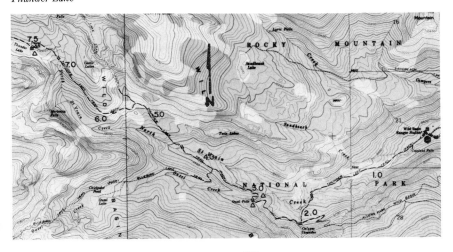

57 BLUEBIRD LAKE

One day trip or backpack
Distance: 7 miles one way
Elevation gain: 2,480 feet
Allow 4 to 4½ hours one way
Usually open July through September
High point: 10,980 feet
Topographic maps:
U.S.G.S. Allens Park, Colo.
7.5′   1957
U.S.G.S. Isolation Peak, Colo.
7.5′   1958

Although not harmonious with the alpine beauty of the terrain surrounding Bluebird Lake, the remains of the massive dam across the lake's outlet are intriguing. The first dam at Bluebird Lake was built in 1902 by a family who operated their ranch on North St. Vrain Creek as a resort. Another, larger dam was constructed from 1912 to 1919 by the second owners of the reservoir.

Turn south from U.S. 34 onto U.S. 36 near the east end of Estes Park. Drive one-half mile then keep right on Colorado 7 and proceed 11 miles to Meeker Park. One and one-half miles farther pass a cluster of buildings where an obscure sign on the left (south) side of the road points to Wild Basin Ranger Station. (The sign, which is easy to miss, is several yards northeast of the small bridge over North St. Vrain Creek.) If you are approaching from the south, drive 8.1 miles north on Colorado 7 from the junction of Colorado 7 and 72. Turn north onto the dirt road and drive past a few buildings then curve left around the east and south shores of Copeland Lake. Continue for two miles to the road's end at a picnic area and the Wild Basin Ranger Station. The trail begins near a large bulletin board you pass on your left as you enter the parking area.

Immediately cross two large bridges then travel at a generally very moderate grade with a few short, gentle stretches of ups and downs. After 0.2 mile pass a sign on your left indicating the path to Copeland Falls and continue along the mostly wooded slope. At 1.8 miles come to an elaborate bridge over North St. Vrain Creek. Climb more noticeably through deeper woods for one-third mile to the junction of the spur to the Finch Lake Trail at Calypso Cascades.

Curve right and cross the complex of streams on three bridges. Although the grade still is irregular, the trail begins climbing more consistently. Three-quarters mile beyond the Cascades pass an outbuilding to your left off the trail just before coming to a sign identifying Ouzel Falls. Cross the stream on a bridge and 200 yards farther come to a viewpoint over the valley and across to Longs Peak and Mt. Meeker. The trail drops to avoid a high rock band then resumes climbing moderately to the junction of the trail to Lion and Thunder Lakes (No's. 55 and 56).

Turn left and climb steeply for a short distance before curving left and rising more moderately along an old road bed. Come to a ridgetop and curve right. Walk along the crest at a very moderate grade and farther on begin traversing along the wooded slope. Resume climbing more noticeably and at 5.3 miles come to the junction of the short spur trail to Ouzel Lake. Keep straight (right) on the main route and continue erratically uphill. Drop slightly and traverse above lily pad-covered Chickadee Pond. Pass through a small boulder field then resume winding up through woods.

Come to a grassy swath below a rock wall and climb through the open area. Above the steep meadow the trail crosses to the other side of a rocky, little canyon and climbs to the edge of a small boulder field. Cross the rubble then reenter vegetation and walk for a few hundred feet to a sign pointing to Bluebird Lake. Turn left and cross Ouzel Creek on a log. Turn right and after several yards resume hiking on a well-defined trail. Wind very steeply up a series of ledges toward the basin that holds Bluebird Lake. After gaining 400 feet of elevation pass a hut on your left and come to the large dam. The slope covered with spires above the lake to the south is the steep, northwestern face of Copeland Mountain.

Ouzel Falls

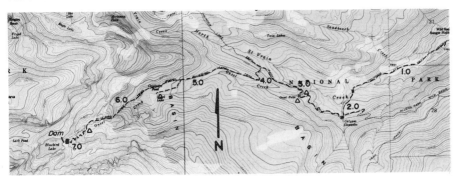

58 FINCH LAKE

One day trip or backpack
Distance: 4.5 miles one way
Elevation gain: 1,660 feet, loss 220 feet
Allow 2½ to 3 hours one way
Usually open late June through September
High point: 10,160 feet
Topographic map:
   U.S.G.S. Allens Park, Colo.
   7.5′   1957

Shore detail at Finch Lake

Several lakes in Rocky Mountain National Park have been named for species of birds found here. Examples include Ouzel, Junco, Pipit, Eagle, Bluebird and Ptarmigan Lakes. Probably the birds you are most likely to see at Finch Lake are the resident Clark Nutcrackers (camp robbers) who aggressively seek to share your lunch.

During portions of the hike to Finch Lake you will have views of Twin Sisters and Pagoda Peaks, Mt. Meeker and the southwest side of Longs Peak. The trail continues two miles beyond Finch Lake and climbs 670 feet to Pear Reservoir. Since the latter is located just below timberline, most of the hike to it is through dense timber.

Turn south from U.S. 34 onto U.S. 36 near the east end of Estes Park. Drive one-half mile then keep right on Colorado 7 and proceed 11 miles to Meeker Park. One and one-half miles farther pass a cluster of buildings where an obscure sign on the left (south) side of the road points to Wild Basin Ranger Station. (The sign, which is easy to miss, is several yards northeast of the small bridge over North St. Vrain Creek.) If you are approaching from the south, drive on Colorado 7 8.1 miles north from the junction of Colorado 7 and 72. Turn north onto the dirt road and drive past a few buildings then curve left around the east and south shores of Copeland Lake. Continue for almost two miles to a sign on your left indicating the mileages to Allens Park and Finch and Pear Lakes. Parking spaces for a few cars are available off the road.

Walk on the level for several yards then curve left and begin a long, steady traverse up the wooded slope of a large lateral moraine. At 0.8 mile come to a clearing at the crest and turn right. Walk through woods of aspen and conifers and after a flat area traverse very gradually downhill to a meadow and the junctions of the trails to Allens Park and Meadow Mountain Ranch.

Keep right on the most northerly trail and walk through a grove of aspen toward the head of the little valley. Reenter the woods and begin climbing. After one set of loose switchbacks traverse along the northern flank of Meadow Mountain several yards uphill from where the slope begins dropping steeply to the valley floor. Walk at a moderate grade then climb more noticeably and come to the junction of trails to Wild Basin Ranger Station and Allens Park. Keep straight and continue climbing. The trail drops slightly then travels along the wooded slope in a series of slight ups and downs. Cross an area of several small streams, the last and largest of which flows throughout the entire summer. After a short distance begin descending and drop for 0.3 mile to the wooded shore of Finch Lake.

Trail near the Allens Park Junction

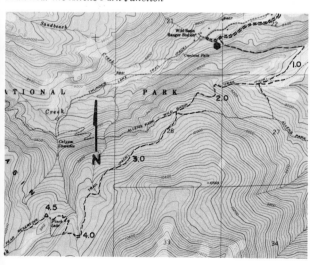

59 BYERS PEAK

One day trip
Distance: 3 miles one way
Elevation gain: 2,255 feet
Allow 2 to 2½ hours one way
Usually open late June through September
High point: 12,804 feet
Topographic maps:
    U.S.G.S. Bottle Pass, Colo.
    7.5′   1957
    U.S.G.S. Byers Peak, Colo.
    7.5′   1957

Byers Peak is the rocky high point on a long massive ridge that stands alone on the western edge of the valley formed by St. Louis Creek and is an easily recognized landmark. The final one-third of the hike climbs above timberline along this ridge to the flat summit that affords extensive views. Especially interesting are the man-made features, including the towns of Fraser and Granby, Lake Granby, Shadow Mountain Reservoir and Williams Fork Reservoir. To the north you can see the western portion of Rocky Mountain National Park and far to the west is the level crest of the Flat Tops. Between you and the southern portion of the Gore Range close to the southwest are the Williams Fork Mountains. The ridges and mountains in the vicinity of Rabbit Ears and Rollins and Berthoud Passes are to the northwest, east and southeast. Carry water as none is available along the climb.

In addition to the trip to Byers Peak, two other excellent trails are near the boundary of the Fraser Experimental Forest: The climb to St. Louis Peak (No. 61) is one and one-half miles longer than the ascent of Byers Peak and travels through a more varied terrain of woods, meadows and high grassy slopes. The trip to St. Louis Peak can be combined with the one to St. Louis Lake (No. 60) or you can make this scenic trek as a separate hike.

Proceed on U.S. 40 to Fraser and near the center of town turn west on Eisenhower Drive where a sign points to Fraser Experimental Forest and St. Louis Creek Campground. After a few blocks turn left, following the route to the Fraser Experimental Forest, and after two miles along a dirt road keep right where a spur goes to St. Louis Creek Campground. Two miles farther turn right at the sign pointing to Byers Peak Trail, keep right again after another two miles and continue the final three miles, negotiating several hairpin switchbacks, to the end of the road. The trail begins on the south side of the turnaround and is marked by a sign.

Traverse up along the densely wooded slope at an erratic, but never steep, grade then begin a steady climb. Cross a large treeless swath and a short distance beyond it at 0.9 mile curve right to the south side of the ridge. Hike near the crest at a gentle grade then near 1.5 miles begin climbing very steeply. Where a faint path goes straight ahead, turn sharply right and continue uphill on the main route. At 1.8 miles come to a little rocky knob at timberline where you will have a good view of the remainder of the route along the grass-covered ridge to the top of the rocky peak. Although the final pitch to the summit looks formidable from here, the ascent actually presents no problems.

Climb along the ridge crest over a series of small humps. Occassionally, the path is faint or stops but the correct route always is obvious and the slopes are covered with grass sod for good footing. The final 0.1 mile of trail winds up the rocky summit to a wooden cross.

The Gore Range from Byers Peak

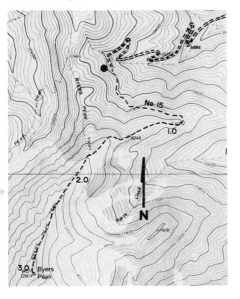

60 ST. LOUIS LAKE

One day trip or backpack
Distance: 3.5 miles one way
Elevation gain: 1,350 feet
Allow 2 hours one way
Usually open late June through September
High point: 11,531 feet
Topographic map:
   U.S.G.S. Byers Peak, Colo.
   7.5′   1957

Camp at St. Louis Lake

The trail to the attractive setting of small St. Louis Lake follows the route to St. Louis Peak (No. 61) for the first two miles then turns north and traverses along a gentle slope through woods and expanses of grass and wild flowers before the final short climb to the tarn. You can make various cross-country explorations from the lake or if you want a more strenuous side trip you could climb to St. Louis Peak. From the lake this ascent would add a total of five miles and 850 feet of elevation gain.

Drive on U.S. 40 to Fraser and near the center of town turn west onto Eisenhower Drive where a sign points to Fraser Experimental Forest and St. Louis Creek Campground. After a few blocks turn left, following the route to the Fraser Experimental Forest, and after two miles along the dirt road keep right where a spur goes to St. Louis Creek Campground. Two miles farther keep left at the junction of the road to Byers Peak Trail then after another two miles keep straight at the side road to Byers Creek Campground and continue the final five miles to the end of the road. A sign across the creek identifies the beginning of the St. Louis Trail.

Cross the stream on a log footbridge and turn left. Climb through woods just above the flow and soon pass through a little grassy valley then wind uphill through a dense stand of timber. Grass and wild flowers grow between the tall evergreens. At 1.7 miles cross St. Louis Creek and walk along a ridge between it and a second stream for 0.1 mile then drop slightly and recross the creek. Hike up through woods for a short distance to an immense meadow and cross to its western edge where a cluster of signs mark the junction of the trail to St. Louis Peak.

Turn right, pass a marker identifying the trail as No. 67, and walk along the west edge of the meadow for 150 yards before reentering woods. Climb steeply for a short distance and make one set of switchbacks. Walk at a very moderate grade through a sparsely wooded area then contour across a gently inclined open slope of grass and wild flowers that extends up to the crest of the ridge above on your left. Resume walking in woods and at 3.0 miles descend into a little side valley, crossing a few small streams, then climb steeply for a short distance up the north slope of the swale. Walk at a considerably more moderate grade through small grassy clearings and clumps of conifers for 0.2 mile. Pass a tarn on your right and after a short climb come to the small bench that holds St. Louis Lake.

Meadow south of the lake

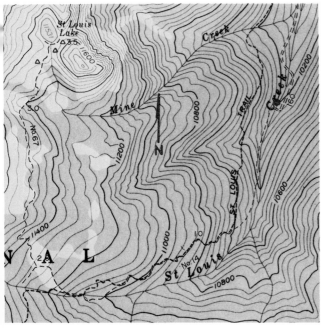

61 ST. LOUIS PEAK

One day trip
Distance: 4.5 miles one way
Elevation gain: 2,295 feet, loss 250 feet
Allow 2½ to 3½ hours one way
Usually open late June through September
High point: 12,246 feet
Topographic map:
U.S.G.S. Byers Peak, Colo.
7.5'   1957

The first half of the hike to St. Louis Peak at the southern tip of the Fraser Experimental Forest is through attractive woods and meadows and the second part climbs along grassy ridges high above timberline. The well-defined trail stops for about one-third mile mid-way along the hike but the route finding here is not especially difficult. If you have some extra time you can make an easy side trip to St. Louis Lake (No. 60). This recommended loop, that travels cross-country across lush grassy slopes, would add negligible elevation gain and three miles to the hike.

Proceed on U.S. 40 to Fraser and near the center of town turn west onto Eisenhower Drive where a sign points to Fraser Experimental Forest and St. Louis Creek Campground. After a few blocks turn left, following the route to the Fraser Experimental Forest, and after two miles along the dirt road keep right where a spur goes to St. Louis Creek Campground. Two miles farther keep left at the junction of the road to Byers Peak Trail then after another two miles keep straight at the side road to Byers Creek Campground and continue the final five miles to the end of the road. A sign across the creek identifies the beginning of the St. Louis Trail.

Cross the stream on a log footbridge and turn left. Climb in woods just above the flow and soon pass through a little grassy valley then continue uphill through a heavy stand of timber. At 1.7 miles cross St. Louis Creek and walk along a ridge between it and a second stream for 0.1 mile then drop slightly and recross the creek. Hike up through woods to an immense meadow and cross to its western edge where signs mark the junction of the trail to St. Louis Lake. In the recommended loop you will return along this route.

Keep left and after a short distance ford St. Louis Creek for a third time. Where the trail becomes faint look first for blazes, then stakes. Carefully note landmarks during the next mile to find the trail on your return if you do not make the loop. Curve to the left and travel up a grassy area near timberline for about 0.1 mile. Meet a well-worn path that traverses south to the saddle on the skyline at 3.0 miles and the junction of the trail to Darling Creek.

Turn left at the saddle and climb along the ridge of grass and scattered rocks. You will have good views to the southwest of the Williams Fork Mountains and beyond them to the Gore Range. Continue up near the crest then descend for 0.3 mile to a saddle. Resume hiking uphill to a cairn and a faint junction. Turn left, leaving the main trail to St Louis Pass, and climb along the ridge for 0.3 mile to the summit.

For the loop to St. Louis Lake, follow the trail down from the saddle at 3.0 miles but instead of turning east after one-half mile continue straight ahead along the slope on the well-worn path. Where the trail becomes faint and finally disappears, continue contouring along the grassy slope. From one rise you will be able to look north and see St. Louis Lake. Begin descending gradually and intersect the main trail then climb to the bench that holds the lake. Return along the route described in the text for No. 60.

St. Louis Peak

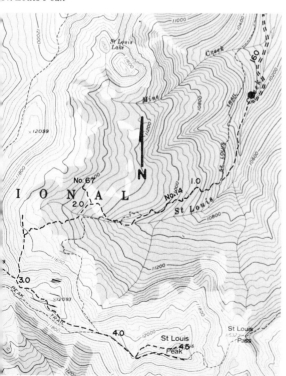

The Gore Range from the ridge west of the Peak

62 PEAK 12,424 (BERTHOUD PASS)

One day trip
Distance: 2 miles one way
Elevation gain: 1,110 feet
Allow 1½ to 2 hours one way
Usually open late June through September
High point: 12,424 feet
Topographic map:
    U.S.G.S. Berthoud Pass, Colo.
    7.5′   1957

Two short trails begin at Berthoud Pass and rise to the summits of nearby unnamed peaks: One heads northeast and travels cross-country to Peak 12,845 (No. 63) and the second, an easier trail described below, heads west along the service road to the upper terminal of a ski lift then after a short, steep climb traverses at a very moderate grade along the rim of a basin. As you follow the crest during the final one-half mile you can look north to the southern portion of Rocky Mountain National Park, west to Byers Peak (No. 59) and Mount Nystrom, east to the Front Range and south as far as Mount Evans. If you want a shorter hike, the crest at 1.5 miles is a good stopping place that offers extensive views. You also can shorten the hike by riding the chair lift that operates for sightseers during the summer season. Carry water as none is available along the climb.

Drive on U.S. 40 to Berthoud Pass and leave your car in the large parking area on the east side of the road southwest of the restaurant and gift shop.

Cross the highway and walk 200 yards southwest of the pass along the shoulder to a dirt road that rises steeply along the grassy, sparsely wooded slope. Climb along this road for two-thirds mile, pass under the chair lift and continue a few hundred feet to the upper terminal. Follow the road beyond the structure for a few feet then turn right onto a faint path. This trail is easy to miss and if you do not locate it just leave the road and continue along the crest in a westerly direction. Soon climb over a small rise on the crest then drop slightly to a small saddle at the base of a very steep slope. The large, yellow circles of alpine sunflower blossoms are scattered along this portion of the trip. Wind up the grass-covered wall toward the ridge top. Although the grade is severe, the footing is good.

At the crest you can look down onto some tarns and across to the remaining route of the hike as it gradually curves west and south along the slope above the basin to Peak 12,424. You can turn and look east across Berthoud Pass to the terrain covered by the hike to Peak 12,845 and to the FAA airway radar station on the summit of Colorado Mines Peak. Turn right and drop slightly then climb over a small hump on the crest. Ascend the slope of grass and rock and continue at a very moderate grade around the rim of the basin to the peak. If you look closely you may be able to spot a ptarmigan camouflaged among the small rocks. These members of the grouse family are white in winter but sport mottled gray feathers during the seasons when the snow cover is gone.

136

Near the summit of the ridge

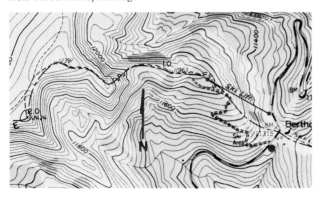

63 PEAK 12,845 (BERTHOUD PASS)

One day trip
Distance: 2.5 miles one way
Elevation gain: 1,630 feet, loss 100 feet
Allow 2 to 2½ hours one way
Usually open late June through September
High point: 12,845 feet
Topographic maps:
    U.S.G.S. Berthoud Pass, Colo.
    7.5'   **1957**
    U.S.G.S. Empire, Colo.
    7.5'   **1958**

The entire climb to this unnamed peak is cross-country and, except for the first quarter mile, is above timberline. The route travels above 12,000 feet for most of the hike but the grade is never severe. Like the neighboring trail that heads west from Berthoud Pass (No. 62), a fine viewpoint can be reached before the actual destination if you want to shorten the trip. From this vantage point at 1.1 miles you can look down onto several tarns on a bench at the head of the valley formed by Blue Creek and from the summit of Peak 12,845 you will be able to see east to the plains, north to Rocky Mountain National Park and south to Mount Evans. Carry drinking water as none is available along the hike.

Proceed on U.S. 40 to Berthoud Pass and leave your car in the large parking area on the east side of the highway southwest of the restaurant and gift shop.

Climb the open slope beside the chair lift that begins at the parking area. Near the top of the lift cross an access road and curve left. After several yards cross a higher road and begin traversing up along the slope. Climb at about a 15 degree angle to the contour. As you gain elevation you will be able to look southwest to the settling ponds of the Urad tungsten mine. Near one-half mile curve around the northern face of Colorado Mines Peak and begin traversing very slightly southeast. You will be able to see the saddle on the skyline to the east that is your immediate destination and you can regulate your rate of climb accordingly. The buildings and other apparatus on the summit of Colorado Mines Peak comprise an FAA airway radar installation.

Turn left at this saddle. You can look down onto the tarns and perhaps be able to spot a few marmots or conies on the rocks below. Walk along the rocky crest near the rim. Like many areas in the northern Colorado Rockies, the small stones scattered over the grass along this section are rich in mica.

Climb over a false summit and at 2.0 miles come to a high point on the ridge. To reach Peak 12,845 turn right and descend in a southeasterly direction to a grassy saddle. Resume climbing and begin traveling over small broken rocks. Pass over a summit then drop a few feet before the last uphill pitch over more broken rocks to a cairn marking the most southerly and highest point on the ridge.

138

Peak 12,845 from the west

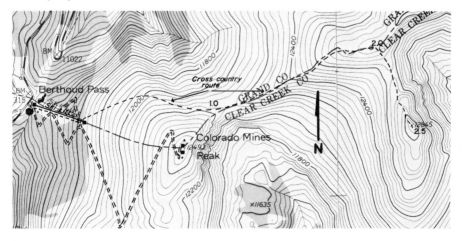

64 CRATER LAKE

One day trip or backpack
Distance: 8.5 miles one way
Elevation gain: 1,970 feet
Allow 4 to 4½ hours one way
Usually open July through September
High point: 10,300 feet
Topographic map:
U.S.G.S. Monarch Lake, Colo.
7.5'   **1958**

Like the other two long hikes described in this guide that climb to the east from the Lake Granby area (No's. 29 and 30), the route to Crater Lake passes through a varied scene of woods, meadows, lakes and rock spires. In addition, at the end of the trip you will have a view of two small glaciers.

If you plan to backpack, an excellent, but strenuous, side trip can be made on the Pawnee Trail which joins at 7.0 miles. You could go only as far as Pawnee Lake or climb another two miles to Pawnee Pass. From there the trail continues down to the exceptionally attractive setting of Lake Isabelle (No. 68).

Drive on U.S. 40 to the west end of Granby and turn north on U.S. 34. Proceed five miles to the junction of Grand County Road 150 at the sign stating Granby Dam and Dikes. (This road is nine miles south of the junction of Colorado 278 and U.S. 34.) Turn east and stay on the main gravel road for nine miles, generally paralleling the southern shore of Lake Granby. At the east end of the lake pass the entrance to Roaring Fork Campground, curve right and continue one mile east to a parking area just before the road is blocked by a gate.

Walk around the gate and continue on the old roadbed for a few hundred feet to a large sign on your left across from the end of Monarch Lake that lists many mileages. (Outhouses are located a few yards northwest of the trailhead.) Hike at a level grade in woods above the north shore of Monarch Lake. Meet the path that follows closer to the shore and continue beyond the lake at a gentle grade near a large meadow. Travel beside Buchanan Creek for a short distance then curve left and head away from the stream. At 1.8 miles come to the junction of the Arapaho Trail.

Keep straight (left) and after several yards make one switchback then continue at a moderate grade through woods. Climb more noticeably and just after coming close to Buchanan Creek a second time begin a series of short switchbacks. Several hundred yards beyond the last one come to a bridge over Hell Creek where a faint path at the west end of the span climbs steeply to a campsite. Contour along the slope at a moderate grade then climb and drop slightly. Walk along an almost level area at the base of a high, rock face and just beyond Shelter Rock Campground come to the junction of the trail to Buchanan Pass. Keep straight (right) and after a short distance cross Buchanan Creek on a large bridge. Climb steeply then switchback up to the left at the edge of the small canyon formed by Cascade Creek. Pass through a small meadow before traversing along the tree and brush-covered valley wall.

Near the head of the valley cross Cascade Creek on a foot log and begin winding up the rock band between the upper and lower valleys. Come to a high waterfall and pool and just beyond them keep right where the trail forks. Soon reach a flat area and re-cross Cascade Creek. Resume climbing, occasionally traveling beside the stream. Walk through an open area of ponds before resuming the traverse up the valley wall.

Enter deep woods and cross Pawnee Creek on foot logs then wind through the forest for a short distance before coming to the junction of the Pawnee Trail. Turn right and travel through woods at an irregular grade for three-quarters mile to a small open area and a third crossing of Cascade Creek. Travel in woods for a few hundred yards then begin climbing in a series of short switchbacks to little Mirror Lake. A sign midway along the west shore identifies Lone Eagle Peak and Fair and Peck Glaciers in the cirques just to the south. Climb slightly, passing a few grass-rimmed tarns, then drop to the north shore of Crater Lake.

Upper Buchanan Creek Valley

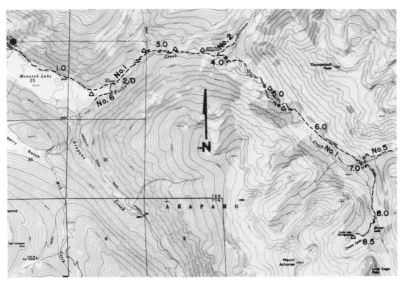

65 COLUMBINE LAKE

One day trip or backpack
Distance: 3 miles one way
Elevation gain: 840 feet
Allow 1½ hours one way
Usually open mid-June through September
High point: 11,060 feet
Topographic map:
    U.S.G.S. Monarch Lake, Colo.
    7.5′   1958

The scenic timberline setting of Columbine Lake is a good choice for a short one day hike or an easy backpack. The grassy little basin south of the lake and the moderate angle of the surrounding rocky slopes provide terrain for explorative walks. If you are doing the trip as a backpack and want a more strenuous trek you could follow the Caribou Trail from the junction at 1.2 miles and climb for three miles and 1,780 feet over Caribou Pass to Arapaho Pass (No. 71). From the latter you can descend along a valley wall then climb to the viewpoint overlooking Arapaho Glacier (No. 70).

Follow U.S. 40 three-quarters mile east of the community of Tabernash or 3.5 miles north of Fraser to a road on the east side of the highway marked by a sign pointing to Devils Thumb Dude Ranch. (This turnoff is about 200 yards south of a long, curving overpass above the railroad tracks.) Turn, leaving the paved surafce, and after 0.1 mile come to a fork. Turn left and 0.4 mile farther where a side road goes to Hurd Creek Ranch keep left again, staying on the main road. After three more miles curve right on the main road and two miles farther keep left and go uphill. Continue one mile to where a side road crosses the main one at a shallow angle. Keep straight (right) then after a short distance pass a large sawdust pile on your left. Three miles from the crossroad keep right at a fork, following the sign pointing to Junco Campground and Caribou Trail. Two-tenths mile beyond the

sign keep left at the marker pointing to Devils Thumb Park and after another 0.2 mile stay left at the edge of a meadow. Drive the final one-half mile to a fork in the road where a sign stating Caribou Trail, Columbine Lake 3 and Arapaho Pass 5 identifies the trailhead. Although level and passable, the last half mile is rough.

Take the old roadbed on the right as indicated by the large sign and the marker on a tree stating Trail 10. Climb very gradually and at 0.5 mile come to a fork. Keep left and after a few hundred feet pass an old log cabin on your right. Continue in woods along the edge of a meadow to the junction of the trail to Arapaho Pass at 1.2 miles. Keep right and a few yards from the fork pass a small marker stating Trail 11. Travel through a meadow on a road for 0.1 mile to the edge of the woods where the trail begins.

Wind up through the deep forest for one-third mile to a long clearing. Walk through the meadow and beyond its far end climb for a short distance to a second, but smaller, grassy area. Climb beside the outlet creek from Columbine Lake then veer left and wind up around boulders and trees. At 2.7 miles cross the stream and briefly continue uphill. Travel at an almost level grade through a grassy, rocky area for several hundred feet, curve left and pass a small marshy area where the trail is faint for a few yards then come to the west shore of Columbine Lake. Surprisingly, the basin above the south end of the lake contains no tarns.

Columbine Lake

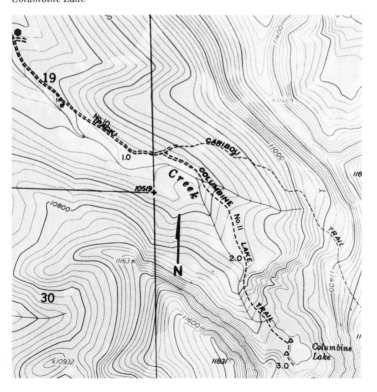

66 MOUNT AUDUBON

One day trip
Distance: 3.5 miles one way
Elevation gain: 2,773 feet
Allow 3 to 4 hours one way
Usually open July through mid-September
High point: 13,223 feet
Topographic map:
   U.S.G.S. Ward, Colo.
   7.5'   1957

Because the summit of Mount Audubon affords such a spectacular view, try to do the climb on a clear, calm day when you can linger on the broad, flat top and enjoy the vista: Longs Peak in Rocky Mountain National Park is in the center of the cluster of summits to the north with Mt. Meeker and Twin Sisters Peaks to its right and Pagoda Peak to the left. The Never Summer Range, the western boundary of the Park, lies to the northwest and beyond to the west and slightly south are Mount Zirkel and Parkview Mountain. Lake Granby and a portion of Middle Park can be seen closer to the west. The Gore Range rises to the southwest and the view south continues down the Front Range to Mount Evans.

Do not attempt the ascent if a thunderstorm is forming as the final two miles is along very exposed terrain. Carry drinking water as the several sources along the hike may not be dependable.

Four of the hikes described in this guide begin at Brainard Lake. The climb to Mount Audubon and the trek along the crest of Niwot Ridge (No. 69) offer panoramic views of the east side of the Front Range and the other two hikes, Mitchell and Blue Lakes (No. 67) and Lake Isabelle and Isabelle Glacier (No. 68), travel along valley bottoms to lake-filled cirques. Because of heavy recreational use, the Forest Service regulates the number of people admitted to the Brainard Lake area between Memorial Day and Labor Day.

Follow Colorado 72 one mile north of the most southerly side road to the town of Ward to a large sign stating Brainard Lake. Turn west and rise along the paved road. After two miles pass the entrance station then continue another 2.5 miles to the west end of Brainard Lake. Turn west at the large sign pointing to Trailhead Parking Area and after 0.2 mile come to a fork. Keep right, following the sign pointing to Mitchell Lake Trailhead Parking, and continue to the end of the road. Signs at the west end of the turnaround identify the trailhead.

Take the path to the right (north), as indicated by the sign stating Mt. Audubon Trail 1½, and walk at a very gradual uphill grade for 100 yards to the junction with a path from the northwest end of the parking area. Turn left and climb through woods at a steady. moderate grade. At 0.6 mile abruptly come to the base of a steep, rocky ridge, turn right and climb to its crest in one set of switchbacks. During this stretch you will be able to see Brainard then Mitchell Lakes and after the trail curves north and begins traversing the east facing slope, the plains and several other lakes come into view. Climb along the rocky trail at a steady, moderate grade, soon rising above timberline At 1.4 miles come to the junction of the Beaver Creek Trail and turn left.

Climb at a gradual grade along the grassy slope. One-half mile from the junction switchback a few times then continue in a westerly direction through several little basins. Just before reaching the crest of the ridge at 3.0 miles enter the beginning of a dense coney population. From here to the summit you will be entertained by these furry little rodents. Turn left and begin winding up over boulders, following the large cairns that have marked the route since the junction at 1.4 miles. After one-half mile come to the northeastern end of the summit and walk south a few yards to a flat area where several stone windbreaks have been constructed.

Peaks southwest of Mt. Audubon

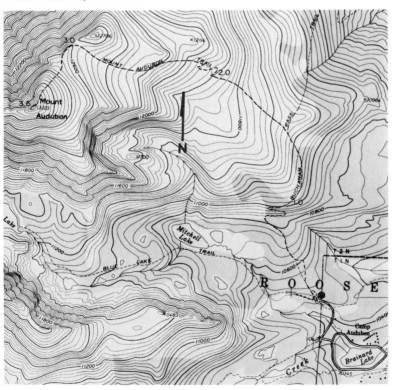

67 MITCHELL AND BLUE LAKES

One day trip or backpack
Distance: 2.5 miles one way
Elevation gain: 850 feet
Allow 1½ to 2 hours one way
Usually open July through September
High point: 11,300 feet
Topographic map:
    U.S.G.S. Ward, Colo.
    7.5′   1957

The trail to Blue Lake begins in deep woods and near the midway point passes through a garden of wild flowers before rising gradually above timberline to the base of Mount Audubon. Experienced hikers can make an enjoyable loop by climbing over the ridge separating Blue Lake and Lake Isabelle (No. 68). Although not steep, a long traverse across a boulder field is necessary on the south side of the ridge. This circuit would add one mile and 500 feet of elevation gain.

Please refer to the third paragraph of Trail No. 66 for information concerning restrictions on the use of trails from Brainard Lake.

Follow Colorado 72 one mile north of the most southerly side road to the town of Ward to a large sign stating Brainard Lake. Turn west and rise along the paved road. After two miles pass the entrance station then continue another 2.5 miles to the western end of Brainard Lake. Turn west at the large sign pointing to Trailhead Parking Area and after 0.2 mile come to a fork. Keep right, following the sign pointing to Mitchell Lake Trailhead Parking, and continue to the end of the road. Signs at the west end of the turnaround identify the trailhead.

Follow the trail to the left as indicated by the sign pointing to Mitchell and Blue Lakes. Walk almost on the level through woods then descend slightly and at 0.4 mile come to the crossing of the exit creek from Mitchell Lake. Begin climbing moderately along the rocky trail then travel at a more gradual grade and come near the end of Mitchell Lake where a side path heads toward the shore. Travel parallel to the south side a few hundred feet from the water and cross one of the inlet creeks that also is the outlet of Blue Lake. Traverse up an open, rock and grass covered slope where you can look down onto Mitchell Lake and a smaller, unnamed lake.

Continue climbing at an erratic, but never steep, grade through an area of grass, scattered trees and wild flowers. Begin traversing a gently sloping valley wall above some tarns. At 2.2 miles curve north into the narrow head of the valley and cross a small side stream near timberline. Walk over slabs and around small rock outcroppings to the eastern shore of Blue Lake. The best campsites are located in the meadow above the falls at the west end of the lake.

To make the cross-country loop to Lake Isabelle, go back along the trail to a point above the outlet end of the large tarn at 2.0 miles. Leave the established route, drop to the valley floor and ford the wide, shallow portion of the stream a short distance below the large tarn. Veer left and climb gradually over grass then curve right so you can continue up on grass to the broad crest. After enjoying the view from the ridge top, drop to a small grassy bench and walk to its southwest edge. Continue downslope, veering slightly to the right. Go across or around a small boulder field then travserse in a westerly direction. Be sure to stay high and do not lose any elevation until you can see Lake Isabelle. Traverse across an immense scree slope to its end, losing as little elevation as possible, then curve left and wind down through woods in a generally southerly direction until you meet the trail to Lake Isabelle.

Blue Lake from Mt. Audubon

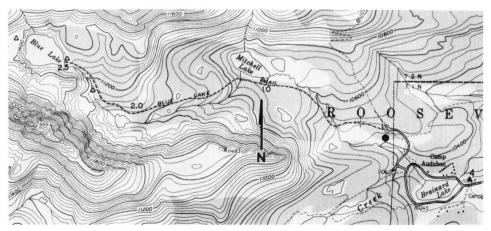

68 LAKE ISABELLE AND ISABELLE GLACIER

One day trip or backpack
Distance: 3.8 miles one way
Elevation gain: 1,550 feet
Allow 2 hours one way
Usually open July through September
High point: 12,000 feet
Topographic maps:
    U.S.G.S. Monarch Lake, Colo.
    7.5′   **1958**
    U.S.G.S. Ward, Colo.
    7.5′   **1957**

Often the most scenic alpine areas are reached only after many miles of hiking, but Lake Isabelle is one of the delightful exceptions. Although located near the head of a basin whose steep, rock walls are topped with immense, jagged pinnacles, the lush patches of grass and trees around the lake greatly soften the setting. A path continues 1.3 miles beyond the lake, passing several tarns, to a viewpoint at the edge of Isabelle Glacier. A strenuous side trip to Pawnee Pass leaves from a junction just below Lake Isabelle.

Please refer to the third paragraph of Trail No. 66 for information concerning restrictions on the use of trails from Brainard Lake.

Follow Colorado 72 one mile north of the most southerly side road to the town of Ward to a large sign stating Brainard Lake. Turn west and climb along the paved road. After two miles pass the entrance station then continue another 2.5 miles to the western end of Brainard Lake. Turn west at the large sign pointing to Trailhead Parking Area and after 0.2 mile come to a fork. Keep left, following the sign pointing to Long Lake Trailhead Parking and continue to the end of the road. A sign near the southwest edge of the turnaround identifies the trailhead.

Walk on the level along the wide, graveled path for one-quarter mile to the junction of the trail to Niwot Ridge (No. 69) just before the northeast tip of Long Lake. Keep straight (right) and continue along the level trail, traveling the length of the lake a short distance from the shore. Beyond the west end walk through deep woods at a very gradual grade. Cross a small stream on logs and continue through the forest before traversing along the edge of a large meadow on the valley floor. At 1.8 miles near the end of the valley switchback several times and come to the junction of the trail to Pawnee Pass. Keep left and climb to a stream. Ford it and travel a short distance to the east end of the lake.

To reach the viewpoint near Isabelle Glacier continue on the path that follows near the northern shore of the lake, climbing slightly and traversing a scree slope at one point. At the end of the lake walk through a little meadow then climb beside the inlet creek for a short distance to a higher and smaller grassy area. The route travels up a miniature canyon of boulders and crosses a small creek. Turn right then left before climbing in several short switchbacks. Continue through a swale of boulders to a tarn. Make several long switchbacks above it then climb into a rocky couloir and traverse up its northern wall before coming near the eastern tip of the glacier.

The trail to Pawnee Pass climbs from the junction near 2.0 miles through woods to a grassy area and crosses a stream on a bridge. Continue up through woods, soon rise above timberline then switchback over rocky slopes to the pass. The climb to the crest would add a total of four miles and 1,640 feet of elevation gain. From the pass the route drops past Pawnee Lake and continues down to a junction with the trail to Crater Lake (No. 64).

Stream near Lake Isabelle

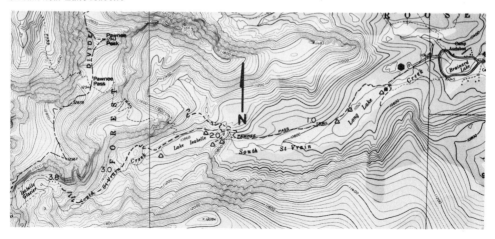

69 NIWOT RIDGE

One day trip
Distance: 4 miles one way
Elevation gain: 1,830 feet
Allow 3 hours one way
Usually open July through September
High point: 12,280 feet
Topographic map:
   U.S.G.S. Ward, Colo.
   7.5′   1957

During the second half of the 1800's Chief Niwot was an important leader of the Southern Arapaho Indians. Because the ends of the fingers on his right hand were missing, he was given this name, the Arapaho word for "left-handed."

Beyond the 1.6 mile point the route travels above timberline over the broad, gentle slopes of Niwot Ridge and during the last one and two-third miles the trail follows an old road bed near the crest where you will be able to look down onto the Green Lakes, part of the water supply for the City of Boulder. Good views of Lake Isabelle and Isabelle Glacier (No. 68) can be enjoyed from the grassy viewpoint at the end of the trek.

Please refer to the third paragraph of Trail No. 66 for information concerning restrictions on the use of trails from Brainard Lake.

Follow Colorado 72 one mile north of the most southerly side road to the town of Ward to a large sign stating Brainard Lake. Turn west and climb along the paved road. After two miles pass the entrance station then continue another 2.5 miles to the western end of Brainard Lake. Turn west at the large sign pointing to Trailhead Parking Area and after 0.2 mile come to a fork. Keep left, following the sign pointing to Long Lake Trailhead Parking, and continue to the end of the road. A sign near the southwest edge of the turnaround identifies the trailhead.

Walk on the level along the wide, graveled path for one-quarter mile to the junction of the trail to Lake Isabelle just before the northeast tip of Long Lake. Turn left, cross the outlet from Long Lake on a bridge and walk along the top of a dike. Curve right and go through a large, grassy area at the edge of the timber. Veer to the left away from the lake and pass a dilapidated cabin on your right. Climb at a moderate, steady grade through deep woods, switchbacking periodically. Several hundred yards beyond a patch of lush vegetation pass through a small open area filled with a considerable variety of wild flowers then wind up a slope covered with rocks and gnarled conifers. As you climb higher you can look down to Brainard Lake then Long Lake and west to the tip of Lake Isabelle. Wend your way through an area of low trees at a very moderate grade. At 1.5 miles leave the stunted timber and 120 yards farther come to the end of the trail at a large cairn. Carefully note the landmarks around this marker so you easily can locate it on your return. Aim for the saddle between the two low summits to the south. As you gradually climb cross-country for the next 0.6 mile you can enjoy both distant views such as Mount Audubon (No. 66) to the northwest and the plains to the east and, considerably closer, the tiny wild flower blossoms splashed across your route.

At the saddle curve right and traverse the slope until you meet an old road and the barbed wire fence that marks the northern boundary of the watershed for the City of Boulder. Follow the road for 1.7 miles near or along the broad, gently rising crest to an experiment station. For the view down onto Lake Isabelle and Isabelle Glacier and across to the slopes near Pawnee Pass continue west from the large cairn at the station along the crest for several hundred feet then turn right and descend the rock and grass covered slope to a stopping place.

Cairn at the end of the trail

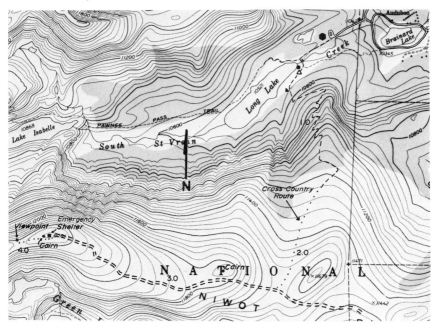

70 ARAPAHO GLACIER

One day trip
Distance: 6 miles one way
Elevation gain: 1,740 feet
Allow 3½ to 4 hours one way
Usually open July through September
High point: 12,700 feet
Topographic maps:
    U.S.G.S. Monarch Lake, Colo.
    7.5′   **1958**
    U.S.G.S. Ward, Colo.
    7.5′   **1957**

Arapaho Glacier lies at the western end of the drainage that serves as the watershed for Boulder, so melt from this ice-field eventually becomes part of the municipality's domestic water supply. Two-thirds of the hike to the base of South Arapaho Peak and the view of the glacier climbs high above timberline along the gentle grassy slopes of a massive ridge. Ambitious hikers can extend the trip by climbing an additional 700 feet to the summit of South Arapaho Peak. Carry drinking water as none is available along the climb.

Drive eight miles north of Nederland or five miles south of Ward on Colorado 72 to a sign stating University of Colorado Mountain Research Station. Turn west onto the dirt road and after 0.8 mile keep left, following the sign to Rainbow Lakes Campground. The road to the trailhead is rough in spots but the grade is never severe. Four miles from the highway keep right where a road goes left to Old Caribou Townsite. Continue one more mile then drive through Rainbow Lakes Campground to its northwestern end and a parking area. A sign marking the beginning of the Glacier Rim Trail is on the north edge of the turnaround.

Traverse up a heavily wooded slope for several hundred yards to a crest and curve slightly left. After a short climb on a rocky tread keep right on the main trail where a faint side path goes left and farther along the route keep right a second time. The trail curves gradually to the northwest as it travels above a broad, wooded valley, paralleling the fence that marks the boundary of the watershed. The very moderate grade is interrupted by only a few slight downhill stretches. At 1.2 miles turn sharply away from the fence, climb more noticeably and begin a series of switchbacks. As you gain elevation, the woods become less dense. Come to a cairn, turn right and continue uphill near timberline for a short distance. Abruptly leave the stunted trees and after a few hundred yards come to the crest of the ridge above the valley that holds Triple, Goose, Island and Silver Lakes. As you continue the hike you will be able to see all of these lakes.

Curve left and climb along the grassy slope. The marshy setting of the Rainbow Lakes can be seen below to the southeast and Niwot Ridge (No. 69) spans the horizon to the north. Where the trail becomes faint turn right and after a few yards resume travelling on the well-worn tread. Traverse above the lake-filled valley in a southwesterly direction for one-half mile then at 3.3 miles begin a set of switchbacks. From the second switchback climb gradually toward the wide saddle on the crest of the ridge. Walk through the saddle and wind up the shoulder of a hump on the crest.

Begin a long, gradual traverse along the southern slope of the ridge. The Lake Eldora Ski Area can be seen to the southeast and closer to the south Diamond Lake (No. 72) perches on a bench. Drop at a moderate grade for one-half mile then resume climbing. Curve to the northwest and begin descending gradually toward the saddle at the base of South Arapaho Peak. After dropping for several hundred yards come to the junction of the trail from the valley floor. This route descends for 1.5 miles to the Fourth of July Mine where it meets the trail to Arapaho Pass (No. 71). Keep right and soon begin the short climb to the Viewpoint. From here you can look southwest down to Arapaho Pass, Dorothy Lake and Mount Neva and beyond them to a portion of the former railroad trestle just below Rollins Pass. The peak to the north with the cairn and cross on its summit is North Arapaho Peak.

South Arapaho Peak

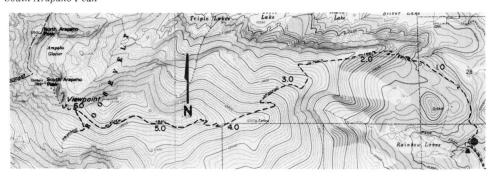

71 ARAPAHO PASS and CARIBOU LAKE

One day trip or backpack
Distance: 4 miles one way
Elevation gain: 1,850 feet, loss 760 feet
Allow 2½ to 3 hours one way
Usually open July through September
High point: 11,906 feet
Topographic maps:
    U.S.G.S. East Portal, Colo.
    7.5'   **1958**
    U.S.G.S. Monarch Lake, Colo.
    7.5'   **1958**

The trail to Arapaho Pass travels through an especially vividly colored garden of wild flowers then at timberline passes the remains of the Fourth of July Mine. You can extend the easy 3.1 mile hike to the pass by making four possible side trips. The shortest is the gradual one-third mile climb to Lake Dorothy at the base of Mount Neva. If you plan to do the hike as a backpack and want a more sheltered campsite you can wind down from the pass for one mile to Caribou Lake. Another mile long trip, but with negligible elevation gain, can be made by following the trail to Caribou Pass northwest of Arapaho Pass. The fourth side trip leaves the main route at 2.0 miles and climbs for 1.5 miles, gaining 1,500 feet of elevation, to the Arapaho Glacier Viewpoint at the base of South Arapaho Peak (No. 70). However, just the moderately graded trail to Arapaho Pass affords a fine hike.

Proceed one mile southwest of Nederland on Colorado 72 to a sign identifying the road to the Eldora Ski Area. Turn right (northwest) and after one mile keep right where a side road on the left climbs to the ski area. Four miles from the highway go through the community of Eldora and begin traveling on a rough dirt road. One mile beyond the settlement keep right, following the sign indicating the route to Buckingham Campground and Arapaho Pass Trail, and four miles farther, beyond the northwest end of the campground, come to a gate across the road. If the few parking spaces here are taken you can drive back along the road and find a spot on the shoulder.

Walk up the road on your right as indicated by the sign stating Diamond Lake, 4th of July Mine and All Trails. Climb moderately for 0.3 mile to a fork where another private side road goes downhill and keep right. Continue uphill for another 0.3 mile to the junction of the route to the Diamond Lake Trail (No. 72). Keep right and climb more steeply along a wide trail. Cross a few streams and, as the trail narrows, begin climbing at a more moderate grade. The woods become sparse and the slopes are covered with gaily colored varieties of wildflowers. Make two short switchbacks and resume traversing along the valley wall, still traveling through a profusion of flowers. At 1.6 miles come to the edge of a bench vegetated with stunted trees and brush and walk across it at a very moderate grade then climb more noticeably for a short distance to the junction of the trail to Arapaho Glacier Viewpoint.

Keep left and just beyond the junction pass the rusted machinery at the site of the Fourth of July Mine several yards off the trail on your right. Climb at a steady, moderate grade along the rocky valley wall for 1.1 miles to Arapaho Pass. At the crest where trails go left and right continue straight for a few yards for a view down to Caribou Lake.

To make the short side trip to Lake Dorothy turn left at the pass and climb moderately for 0.3 mile. Where you reach the level of the lake leave the trail and walk cross-country to the shore. If you plan to make the side trip to Caribou Pass, continue along the main trail that passes near Lake Dorothy. Descending from the pass for 1.7 miles will take you to the junction with the trail to Columbine Lake (No. 65). To reach Caribou Lake, follow the trail that goes northeast from Arapaho Pass and climb a short distance then begin winding down for three-quarters mile to the floor of the marshy, grassy basin.

Caribou Lake

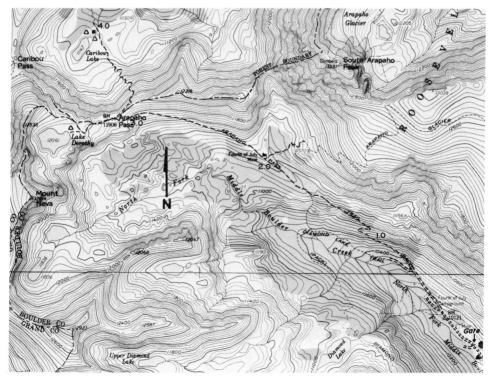

72 DIAMOND LAKE

One day trip or backpack
Distance: 2.5 miles one way
Elevation gain: 890 feet
Allow 1 hour one way
Usually open July through September
High point: 10,950 feet
Topographic maps:
   U.S.G.S. East Portal, Colo.
   7.5'   1958
   U.S.G.S. Monarch Lake, Colo.
   7.5'   1958

Many fine camping sites will be found in the meadows and wooded areas along the shore of Diamond Lake, but whether you take one or more days for this hike, you are urged to continue the trek for an additional 1.5 miles and 350 feet of elevation gain to the overlook above Jasper Lake. This side trip traverses a steep, wooded valley wall then climbs through fields of grass and wild flowers to the crest of a broad, treeless ridge.

Drive one mile southwest of Nederland on Colorado 72 to a sign identifying the road to the Eldora Ski Area. Turn right (northwest) and after one mile keep right where a side road on the left climbs to the ski area. Four miles from the highway go through the community of Eldora and begin traveling on a rough dirt road. One mile beyond the settlement keep right, following the sign indicating the route to Buckingham Campground and Arapaho Pass Trail, and four miles farther, beyond the northwest end of the campground, come to a gate across the road. If the few parking spaces here are taken you can drive back along the road and find a spot on the shoulder.

Walk up the road on your right as indicated by the sign stating Diamond Lake, 4th of July Mine and All Trails. Climb moderately for 0.3 mile to a fork where another private road goes downhill and keep right. Continue uphill for another 0.3 mile to the junction of the route to Arapaho Pass (No. 71). Keep left on the road and soon resume climbing at a gradual grade. A sign marking the Diamond Lake Trail is one mile from the junction.

Turn left onto the path and descend gradually for a few hundred feet to a log crossing over the North Fork of Middle Boulder Creek. Wind up through woods, frequently passing patches of grass and wild flowers. Many side paths diverge from the trail but they eventually rejoin the main route. Begin rising more noticeably and at 2.2 miles come to the north edge of the bench that holds Diamond Lake. Travel on the level through a meadow to a strip of trees and come to a sign at a fork. Keep right and walk for a few hundred feet to the lake.

To make the highly recommended side trip, keep left at the fork just before Diamond Lake and after a short distance ford the exit creek. Climb several yards up the little slope on the south side of the stream in the same direction you had been traveling before the crossing. Bear left and travel through a small swale. Look for a faint tread and an obelisk-shaped cairn at the northeast edge of the swale. Go around the face of the ridge then traverse along a well-defined path at an erratic grade. Pass through a few small marshy areas and at the far edge of the last one turn sharply right and climb steeply for a short distance. Continue uphill, leaving the timber, and enter a broad, grassy side valley. At a cairn where the trail becomes faint curve left and follow more markers. The path becomes obvious again and winds up to the ridge crest. From here you can look north to Arapaho Glacier Viewpoint (No. 70) at the base of South Arapaho Peak.

Turn right and contour along the slope, following cairns at first then a well-defined path. To reach the overlook, stay on the trail for a short distance as it curves left then leave the established route and climb to a saddle. Drop along the grassy slope until you are able to look down onto Jasper Lake. If you want to follow the trail down to the lake (a loss of 500 feet and an additional two miles), continue contouring on the faint trail — do not leave it and climb to the saddle. Follow the cairns down to the timber, cross a burned area then go downhill to the shore. The trail continues from Jasper Lake to Devils Thumb Lake then climbs to the Corona Trail (No. 73).

South Arapaho Peak

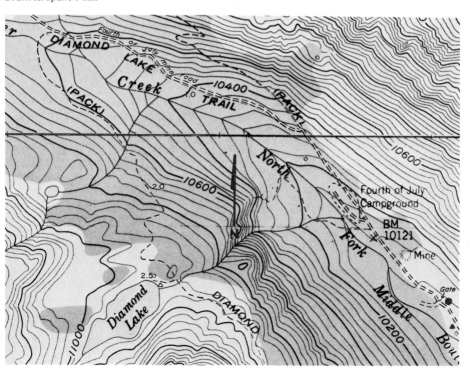

73 CORONA TRAIL

One day trip or backpack
Distance: 3.7 miles one way to
Devils Thumb Lake
Elevation gain: 380 feet, loss 1,040 feet to
Devils Thumb Lake
Allow 2½ to 3 hours one way to Devils Thumb
Lake
Usually open July through mid-September
High point: 12,000 feet
Topographic map:
U.S.G.S. East Portal, Colo.
7.5′   1958

The drive to Corona Trail is almost as exciting as the hike. The road follows the railroad grade that wound over Rollins Pass from 1904 until 1929. Your trip along this historic route will be even more enjoyable if you have the pamphlet *The Moffat Road* available from the Arapaho and Roosevelt National Forests.

Most of the hike is a very gradual traverse along high, tundra slopes that offer extensive views of the broad Fraser Valley 4,000 feet below. The pass at 2.7 miles is a good place to stop if you want an easy trip but you can wind down from the notch an additional mile to Devils Thumb Lake for a more strenuous trek or to find a campsite.

A loop is possible by returning cross-country to Bob and Betty Lakes then following the trail from the latter past King Lake (No. 74) to the starting point at Rollins Pass. This circuit would add no mileage and 700 feet of elevation gain.

From the east, proceed on Colorado 119 or Colorado 72 to Rollinsville and turn west onto a dirt road. Follow the road 6.5 miles, through Tolland to a sign listing several mileages, and 0.1 mile beyond it keep right where a spur goes left to the East Portal of Moffat Tunnel. Drive along the narrow road for 15 miles to Rollins Pass. From the west, drive on U.S. 40 one mile north of the turnoff to Winter Park or 1.5 miles south of Hideaway Park to a sign on the east side of the highway marking the beginning of the Corona Pass Road. Follow this dirt road and after eight miles turn up to the right at a sign stating Old Railroad Bed then six miles farther come to the pass. Turn northwest from the road and park near the foundation of the restaurant-hotel that once stood here.

Walk along the most westerly of the roads that head north from the foundation for 0.2 mile then drop to a saddle and the junction of the trail to King Lake. Keep left and as you wind up the slope above the saddle you can look down to King and Betty Lakes and southwest to the Winter Park Ski Area. At the crest follow the large cairns across the tundra. Soon the trail again becomes obvious and farther on where several routes parallel each other, follow the highest one, as marked by the tall cairns. At 1.4 miles curve right around the face of the broad, gentle slope and head in a northeasterly direction at the same gradual grade. Leave the increasingly faint trail and drop slightly to avoid some fingers of rock then climb northeast toward the pass on the skyline at the base of a slope that rises to the north from the notch. The sign at the gap states Devils Thumb Pass but, actually, the real one is 0.5 mile to the north. Walk several yards to the east end of the pass for a view down onto Devils Thumb and Jasper Lakes.

To reach Devils Thumb Lake, descend along the crest of a narrow ridge then switchback down a slope. Pass a large, shallow tarn and walk through grass and trees to the campsites at the southeast end of the lake. The trail continues down the valley for one mile to Jasper Lake then climbs to Diamond Lake (No. 72).

To make the loop, climb south from the pass toward the rim and walk south near the edge above two cirques. Where you come to the third cirque descend the grassy slope on the north wall. Although steep, the footing is good. Stay on the left (east) side of the couloir and pass a small mine shaft. Keep high, trying not to lose much elevation, and curve to the left then aim for the bench above Bob Lake (also called Cliff Lake). Where you are above the north end of the lake begin dropping gradually and come to the southeast shore.

Pumphouse Lake and the Rollins Pass Road

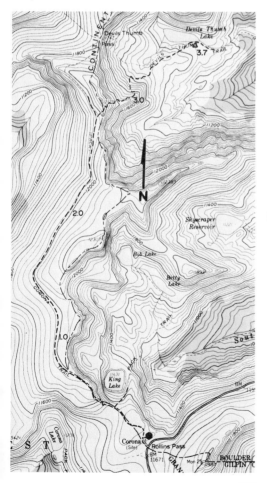

Sign at the pass above Devils Thumb Lake

74 KING, BETTY AND BOB LAKES

One day trip or backpack
Distance: 1.8 miles one way
Elevation gain: 450 feet, loss 550 feet
Allow 1 hour one way
Usually open July through mid-September
High point: 11,750 feet
Topographic map:
    U.S.G.S. East Portal, Colo.
    7.5′   1958

The west and east sides of the ridge that runs north from Rollins Pass offer a dramatic contrast in terrain. The gently inclined, grassy west slope continues up to the broad, flat crest of the ridge then ends abruptly at the rim of the rocky eastern wall that drops precipitously for several thousand feet. An uninterrupted expanse of tundra carpets this relatively smooth western side but on the eastern half a series of lake-filled cirques form indentations along the base of the almost vertical walls and benches covered with grass, brush and stunted trees create a terraced effect on the basin floor. The Corona Trail (No. 73) traverses the gentle western side of the Continental Divide and the trail to King, Betty and Bob Lakes travels through the basin.

The route beyond King Lake is not always obvious and the 0.3 mile between Betty and Bob Lakes is easy cross-country travel. An interesting loop trip combines this trek with the hike along the Corona Trail. Although you can make the circuit in either direction, probably the route finding is a little easier by visiting King, Betty and Bob Lakes first. This would involve no additional elevation gain and only one extra mile of travel.

If you are approaching from the east, drive on Colorado 119 or Colorado 72 to the community of Rollinsville and turn west onto a dirt road, following the sign pointing to Tolland and East Portal. Travel along the valley floor for 6.5 miles to a large sign listing several mileages and one-tenth mile beyond it keep right where a spur goes left to the east end of the Moffat Tunnel. Climb along the narrow former railroad grade for

15 miles to Rollins Pass. Coming from the west, drive on U.S. 40 one mile north of the turnoff to Winter Park or 1.5 miles south of Hideaway Park to a sign on the east side of the highway marking the beginning of the Corona Pass Road. (Although Rollins Pass is the official name, the station, hotel, restaurant and other buildings comprising the small community at the crest was called Corona, the Spanish word for crown, so the pass also is known by that name.) Follow the dirt road and after eight miles turn up to the right at a sign stating Old Railroad Bed then six miles farther come to the pass. Turn northwest from the road and park near the foundation of the restaurant-hotel that once stood here.

Walk along the most westerly of the roads that head north from the foundation for 0.2 mile then drop to a saddle and the junction of the Corona Trail. From here you will be able to look down over much of the terrain covered by the hike to the lakes. Turn right and traverse down the slope above King Lake. Wind down from the bench that holds the circular lake and continue dropping to a stream crossing at 1.1 miles. Just beyond the creek keep left on a faint path and follow along the stream bed for a few yards. Veer right and continue climbing along the rocky crest above the timber to the southeastern end of Betty Lake.

To reach Bob Lake (called Cliff Lake by oldtimers familiar with the area) hop across the outlet creek from Betty Lake and continue along the southwest shore then begin to climb. Keep the outlet creek from Bob Lake on your right and go through two little depressions before coming to the south shore.

To make the recommended loop, cross the exit creek from Bob Lake and wind up in a northeasterly direction to a bench. Veer left and climb moderately then curve right into the grassy couloir above the north end of the lake. Pass an abandoned mine shaft and climb steeply to the rim. Continue north near the edge past two cirques then traverse down to the pass described in Trail No. 73.

160

King and Bob Lakes

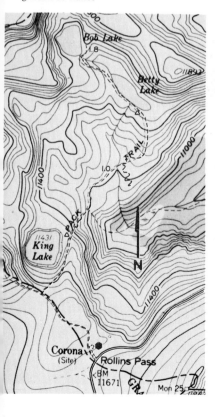

75 ARAPAHO LAKES

One day trip or backpack
Distance: 3.6 miles one way
Elevation gain: 2,050 feet
Allow 3 to 3½ hours one way
Usually open July through September
High point: 11,200 feet
Topographic map:
    U.S.G.S. East Portal, Colo.
    7.5′   1958

Four scenic hikes, all to lakes situated below the steep, eastern face of the Continental Divide, begin from the east end of the Moffat Tunnel. The lakes are near or above timberline and side trips of varying difficulty can be made from each one. The visit to Crater Lakes (No. 76) is the shortest and easiest of the four and hardy hikers can do the trek to the grassy shore of Heart Lake (No. 78) as a loop trip. All the trails have a few steep uphill stretches in woods and the climb to Arapaho Lakes involves about 0.5 mile of easy cross-country travel. Route finding to Clayton and Iceberg Lakes (No. 77) is considerably more challenging.

If you camp at Arapaho Lakes and want to explore, try Forest Lakes to the north. Despite several signs a trail no longer is maintained to Forest Lakes from East Portal. (However, the lake is accessible by a short trail from the road over Rollins Pass.)

Proceed on Colorado 119 or Colorado 72 to the community of Rollinsville and turn west onto a dirt road, following the sign identifying the route to Tolland and East Portal. After 6.5 miles pass a large sign listing several mileages. One-tenth mile beyond it turn left at the sign pointing to East Portal. Drive 1.5 miles to the large parking area near the east end of the Moffat Tunnel. Space for many cars is available north of the tracks.

Walk across the railroad tracks and the bridge then climb over a metal gate. Curve right and continue 200 yards to a fence and signs that mark the beginning of the South Boulder Trail. Go through the fence and hike along a scenic old road bed through meadows and woods. Pass some cabins and continue along the road at a very moderate grade, making an easy ford near 0.5 mile. Begin climbing more noticeably and come to a large clearing and the junction of the trail to Heart, Clayton, Iceberg and Crater Lakes.

Turn right and climb along an old road bed at a steady, moderate grade. Continue traversing the wooded slope and 0.6 mile from the junction ford large Arapaho Creek. Although there is no bridge over the flow, the crossing is not too difficult. Climb steeply for a short distance then resume hiking at a more moderate grade. Continue along the road through woods and open areas of grass and flowers with moderate ups and downs then at 2.7 miles bear left at a faint fork in the road and recross Arapaho Creek. Walk on the level for several hundred yards then begin winding up steeply through woods, following a use path. Keep the stream on your right — do not cross it. After climbing for 0.3 mile leave the woods and come to a grass covered rock band on your right. The well-defined trail stops here.

Continue in the direction you had been traveling and walk along the base of the slope for 100 yards then curve right into a little swale. Bear slightly right and climb along the slope over the wooded crest at the head of the small valley. Drop along a path to the end of a pond. Keep left and walk around the south and west shores to a small ridge between this and a second tarn. You also can reach the ponds by turning right where you first come to the rock band. Climb the low slope then drop, bearing slightly left, to a pond and walk along its southern shore to the low, little ridge. Turn west at the grassy area between the two ponds and climb a rocky, grassy couloir, gaining about 400 feet of elevation. At the crest immediately start bearing left and walk over mostly level terrain covered with stunted trees and large stones for about 75 yards before dropping to the largest of the Arapaho Lakes. The few campsites are located above the eastern shoreline.

F.A.A. Airway beacon above the lakes

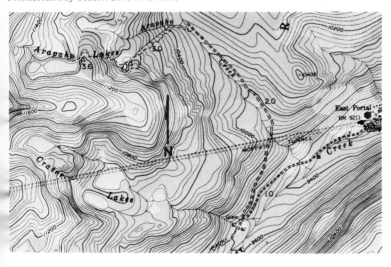

76 CRATER LAKES

One day trip or backpack
Distance: 3 miles one way
Elevation gain: 1,790 feet
Allow 2 hours one way
Usually open July through September
High point: 11,600 feet
Topographic map:
   U.S.G.S. East Portal, Colo.
   7.5′   **1958**

The grass and tree-rimmed south shore of the largest of the three Crater Lakes is an attractive destination for a short hike or an easy backpack. A demanding cross-country trip that would add one-half mile and 400 feet of elevation gain is possible by climbing to the highest of the Crater Lakes.

Although apparent only by looking at a map, the route of the Moffat Tunnel is underneath the northern end of the largest of the Crater Lakes. When David Moffat, a Denver banker, had the railroad route over Rollins Pass built in 1904 he intended to use it only for the few years it would take to build a tunnel under the Continental Divide. However, resistance from the two established railroads to the north and south delayed construction of the tunnel until 1923. Completed in 1927, the tunnel cost $18,000,000 and the lives of 19 workers. But trains that took 2½ hours to cross Rollins Pass from Tolland to Georgetown then could travel the 6.21 miles under the range in twelve minutes.

Drive on Colorado 119 or Colorado 72 to the community of Rollinsville and turn west onto a dirt road, following the sign identifying the route to Tolland and East Portal. Proceed along the broad valley floor and after 6.5 miles pass a large sign listing several mileages. One-tenth mile beyond it turn left at the sign pointing to East Portal. Drive 1.5 miles to the large parking area near the east end of the Moffat Tunnel. Space for many cars is available north of the tracks.

Walk across the railroad tracks and the bridge then climb over a metal gate. Curve right and continue 200 yards to a fence and signs that mark the beginning of the South Boulder Trail. Go through the fence and hike along a scenic old road bed through meadows and woods. Pass some cabins and continue along the road at a very moderate grade, making an easy ford near 0.5 mile. Begin climbing more noticeably and come to a large clearing and the junction of the trail to Arapaho Lakes (No. 75).

Keep straight (left) and continue through the meadow, passing the ruins of two buildings. Reenter woods and resume climbing. Where the trail forks, you can follow either branch, although the one to the left does have a smoother surface. Begin rising at a steeper grade and where you come to a side path to the right marked by green spray, keep left on the main trail. Continue climbing to the junction of the trail to Heart Lake (No. 78).

Although the sign at this junction states the route to Crater Lakes is cross-country, the trail actually is well-defined and easy to follow. Turn right and after 150 feet keep left on the rocky trail where a side path continues straight. Soon begin climbing very steeply along the rough surface of exposed roots and rocks. Curve gradually to the northwest for one-third mile from the junction then begin traveling at a more moderate grade in a northerly direction. After an almost level section climb for a short distance then drop and walk at an irregular grade to an open grassy area. Cross the creek, turn left and walk about 100 feet to the eastern end of the most southerly Crater Lake. To reach the largest lake, head north from the ford and walk 200 yards to the southern bank. Several good campsites are located along the southwestern shore.

Camp at Crater Lakes

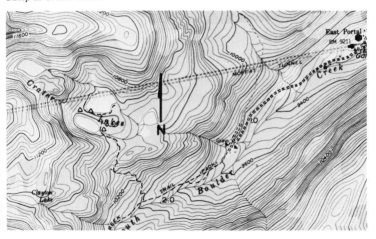

77 CLAYTON AND ICEBERG LAKES

One day trip or backpack
Distance: 4.5 miles one way
Elevation gain: 2,640 feet
Allow 3½ to 4 hours one way
Usually open July through September
High point: 11,850 feet
Topographic map:
    U.S.G.S. East Portal, Colo.
    7.5′   1958

Hikers and backpackers who enjoy the challenge of steep, faint paths and difficult route finding will want to make the trip to Clayton and Iceberg Lakes. The sometimes obscure path to the former leaves a well-defined trail at 2.5 miles and for one-third mile climbs beside a cascade, occasionally at a 30 degree angle. The trail stops entirely at Clayton Lake and the remaining 1.5 miles to either north or south Iceberg Lake is cross-country up a scenic but rugged alpine valley of rock bands and grassy benches. If you are backpacking and do not want to negotiate the steep climb with a heavy load, you could make a loop by visiting Heart Lake (No. 78) first. See the text of that trail for a description of the terrain between Heart Lake and the valley below the Iceberg Lakes.

Proceed on Colorado 119 or Colorado 72 to the community of Rollinsville and turn west onto a dirt road, following the sign identifying the route to Tolland and East Portal. Drive along the broad valley floor and after 6.5 miles pass a large sign listing several mileages. One-tenth mile beyond it turn left at the sign pointing to East Portal. Drive 1.5 miles to the large parking area near the east end of the Moffat Tunnel. Space for many cars is available north of the tracks.

Walk across the railroad tracks and the bridge then climb over a metal gate. Curve right and continue 200 yards to a fence and signs that mark the beginning of the South Boulder Trail. Go through the fence and hike along a scenic old road bed through meadows and woods. Pass some cabins and continue along the road at a very moderate grade, making an easy ford near 0.5 mile. Begin climbing more noticeably and come to a large clearing and the junction of the trail to Arapaho Lakes (No. 75).

Keep straight (left) and continue through the meadow, passing the ruins of two buildings. Reenter woods and resume climbing. Where the trail forks, you can follow either branch, although the one to the left does have a smoother surface. Begin rising at a steeper grade and where you come to a side path to the right marked by green spray, keep left on the main trail. Continue climbing to the junction of the trail to Crater Lakes (No. 76) and keep left. Walk at a more moderate grade for 0.2 mile to a sign marking the junction of the Iceberg Lakes Cutoff. The main trail continues to Heart Lake.

Turn right and wind up through woods at a moderate grade, generally traveling near the outlet creek from Clayton Lake. Near the base of a high rock bluff veer left through a small boulder field then climb very, very steeply between the stream and the vertical southern end of the rock wall. At the top of the bluff the grade becomes more moderate and the trail heads away from the creek. Just below Clayton Lake leave the timber and climb steeply along an open slope then traverse above the wooded northern shore.

To reach the Iceberg Lakes, continue west from Clayton Lake, staying on the north side of the inlet stream. At 4.0 miles, after the first scramble up to a bench, curve left and wind your way up the main valley to reach the most southerly of the lakes which indeed is covered with ice floes most of the summer. The route is dotted with fine specimens of arctic gentian whose blossoms are a speckled, greenish-white instead of the more familiar deep blue. The most direct route to the northern lake is to keep right at 4.0 miles and continue straight up the slope.

South Iceberg Lake

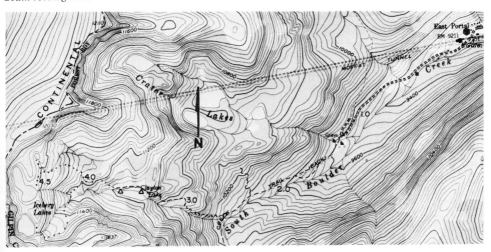

78 HEART LAKE

One day trip or backpack
Distance: 5 miles one way
Elevation gain: 2,090 feet
Allow 2½ to 3 hours one way
Usually open July through September
High point: 11,300 feet
Topographic map:
    U.S.G.S. East Portal, Colo.
    7.5′   1958

Heart Lake lies in a large grassy basin just above timberline and several side trips can be made from here. The main trail continues one mile up to Rogers Pass, 560 feet above Heart Lake on the Continental Divide, or a short side path drops to the little valley below Heart Lake that holds Rogers Pass Lake. An exceptionally scenic trip is the easy cross-country hike to the overlook above the most southerly of the two Iceberg Lakes. A moderately difficult loop trip is possible by descending from this viewpoint and returning to the main trail by way of Clayton Lake (No. 77). Some route finding problems occur on this circuit and one section of the trail below Clayton Lake is extremely steep, but the adventurous hiker will enjoy these challenges.

Drive on Colorado 119 or Colorado 72 to Rollinsville and turn west onto the dirt road to Tolland and East Portal. After 6.5 miles pass a large sign listing several mileages. One-tenth mile beyond it turn left and drive 1.5 miles to the parking area near the east end of the Moffat Tunnel. Space for many cars is available north of the tracks.

Walk across the railroad tracks and the bridge then climb over a metal gate. Curve right and continue 200 yards to a fence and signs that mark the South Boulder Trail. Go through the fence and hike along a scenic old road bed through meadows and woods. Pass some cabins and continue along the road at a very moderate grade, making an easy ford near 0.5 mile. Begin climbing more noticeably and come to a large clearing and the junction of the trail to Arapaho Lakes (No. 75).

Keep straight (left) and continue through the meadow, passing the ruins of two buildings. Reenter woods and resume climbing. Where the trail forks, follow either branch, although the left path is smoother. Begin rising at a steeper grade and where you come to a side path to the right marked by green spray, keep left on the main trail. Continue climbing to the junction of the trail to Crater Lakes (No. 76) and keep left. Walk at a more moderate grade for 0.2 mile to a sign marking the junction of the Iceberg Lakes Cutoff. You will return by this path if you make the possible loop.

Again keep left and cross a stream. Continue at a moderate grade and follow a circuitous route around blowdown then near 3.6 miles begin climbing very steeply. Eventually, the grade is less severe. Come to a small grassy area and beyond it traverse up the open southern slope of a little valley. Pass the side trail that drops for one-half mile with an elevation loss of 100 feet to Rogers Pass Lake. Keep right and continue climbing for a short distance to a level area of brush and grass where the trail stops. Walk in a westerly direction, heading toward the trail that can be seen winding up the slope to Rogers Pass. Do not cross the outlet creek. Eventually, you probably will resume traveling on a well-defined path for a short distance then curve right and walk to the southern end of Heart Lake.

To make the cross-country side trip to the viewpoint above Iceberg Lake, cross the outlet creek from Heart Lake and climb the grass and rock covered slope to a low saddle above the northeast end of Heart Lake. From this crest drop slightly and climb to another crest to the north. The going is easy and you may be fortunate enough to see some conies or a ptarmigan hen and her chicks. Where you reach the broad plateau continue northwest a short distance for a view of the most southerly Iceberg Lake. If you are making the loop trip, bear right at the crest and walk northeast until you reach a less steep part of the grassy slope below to the north. Wind down through exceptional displays of arctic gentian into the valley and proceed east as described in the text for Trail No. 77.

Heart Lake

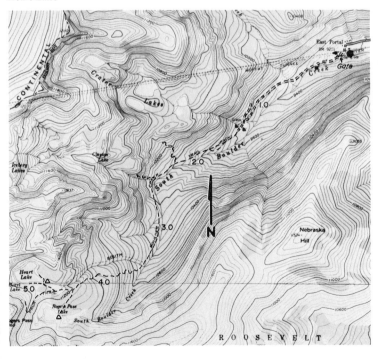

79 GREYROCK MOUNTAIN

One day trip or backpack
Distance: 3 miles one way
Elevation gain: 2,115 feet
Allow 2½ to 3 hours one way
Usually open May through October
High point: 7,613 feet
Topographic map:
    U.S.G.S. Poudre Park, Colo.
    7.5′   1962

Even after being informed what to expect, the climb to the summit of Greyrock Mountain is still a series of delightful surprises: Instead of traversing the arid, barren slopes you would expect to find along the route, most of the trail travels under the shade of conifers. Then near 1.6 miles where you see the impressive dome of Greyrock Mountain for the first time you only can ask, "How can any hiking trail reach the top of *that?*" This query is answered after a steep, but never exposed, climb and there below the rocky summit, just as the map shows, is a lake. The Greyrock Trail was built in the 1930's by Civilian Conservation Corps.

The climb is best done in the fall or late spring as summertime temperatures are very high. (If you do make the hike in summer, watch for rattlesnakes.) Carry water as none safe for drinking is available.

Proceed about 10 miles west of Fort Collins on U.S. 287 to the junction with Colorado 14 at Ted's Place. Turn left onto Colorado 14 and drive nine miles to a sign on your right pointing to Greyrock Mountain 3. Parking space for two cars is available on the shoulder near the sign and another wide spot is located 150 feet back along the highway.

Descend for several feet and cross the Cache La Poudre River on a large bridge. Turn left and travel parallel to the river for a short distance before entering woods and starting to climb moderately. Walk along the floor of a small valley then at 0.7 mile turn sharply up to the right at a sign pointing to Greyrock Trail and climb along an open slope for a few hundred yards, passing under power lines. Reenter woods and traverse near the floor of a narrow canyon, crossing from one side to the other at one point and making a few short switchbacks. Walk on the level by a small meadow then resume climbing. Near the head of the valley begin rising in a series of switchbacks.

At 1.6 miles traverse at a quite moderate grade along a less densely wooded slope that soon affords views of Greyrock Mountain ahead to the north and a valley of rock outcroppings below to the west. Climb steeply for a short distance to a large, flat grassy area at the base of the dome. Curve right and drop very slightly. Climb along the wooded southeastern slope of the mountain and soon start rising at a considerably steeper grade. Begin descending and after walking downhill for about 50 feet look for a circle of orange spray paint on a huge boulder to your left. Turn left and wind up for 200 feet to a level area. Curve right as indicated by rock arrows and walk along the slabs for 100 feet to a cairn. Turn left and resume winding up. Come to the edge of a grassy, rock-rimmed basin, cross through the center of the meadow and keep on the trail as you reenter woods and curve to the left. Walk through trees for a short distance then wind up around rocks to the unnamed lake.

To reach the top, keep left and scramble up along the south side of the summit block. From the small, rocky perch at the crest you can look directly below to the meadow at the base of the dome and southeast to the glittering buildings of Fort Collins at the edge of the plains. The peaks of the Front Range in the northern-most section of Rocky Mountain National Park line the horizon to the southwest and more mountains fill the scene to the west and northwest.

Hikers at the Lake

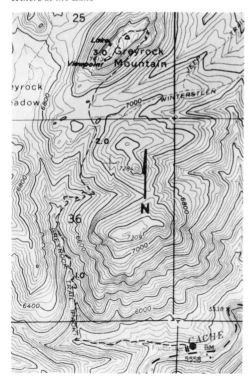

Summit of Greyrock Mountain

80 ROYAL ARCH

One day trip
Distance: 1.5 miles one way
Elevation gain: 600 feet, loss 100 feet
Allow 1¼ hours one way
Usually open March through November
High point: 6,850 feet
Topographic map:
    U.S.G.S. Eldorado Springs, Colo.
    7.5′   **1965**

Rising abruptly from the southwestern city limits of Boulder is a 3,000 foot high band of hills collectively called the Flatirons. Actually, the geological term "flatiron" refers to the large, tilted rock outcroppings protruding from the slope. The Flatirons are composed of material eroded from the range that existed before the present Rockies. Although all this strata that formed the foothills of the Front Range subsequently were uplifted and tilted at the same time, the Flatirons and a few other formations farther south stand out because of their greater resistance to erosion. The biogeography of the area is as interesting as its geomorphology: The shade on the steep east side and the moist conditions close to the high Flatirons combine to create a satisfactory environment for plants not usually found in semi-arid regions. Additionally, because of the steepness of the slopes plants from several zones grow relatively close together.

The precipitous, heavily-vegetated area surrounding the Flatirons is part of 6,000 acre Boulder Mountain Park that extends south along the foothills of the Front Range. The Park is penetrated by a network of trails and the possible outings range from easy strolls to technical rock climbs. The short, but often steep, trail to Royal Arch is one of the more demanding hikes. Along this trek, which generally travels through dense stands of timber, you will have views of Boulder and at the destination, directly under the span of Royal Arch, of the plains to the south and east. After this trip you probably will want to explore more of the area. Carry water as no dependable supply is available along the climb.

Drive to Boulder and proceed south to the intersection of 9th Street and Baseline Road. Continue a very short distance west on Baseline Road to the first road on your left. Turn left (south) here then after several yards keep straight on the road that passes a large sign. Travel one-third mile on a paved road then continue on a dirt surface for the final one-half mile to the turn-around and parking area at Bluebell Shelter. The trail begins south of the structure a few yards down the road from the large diagrammatic sign at the southwest crest of the turnaround.

Drop several yards, passing a sign stating Royal Arch, then climb for about 100 feet. Periodically, you will see color-coded wooden markers tacked on trees identifying the route. Keep left where the trail forks and descend then climb for 40 feet. The trail rises at a steady grade through a park-like setting of widely spaced trees and sparse ground cover near the edge of a small canyon. Traverse along an open slope just before crossing to the opposite side of the canyon at 0.5 mile. Enter dense deciduous woods and climb moderately steeply along the wall. The broad tilted face of the largest Flatiron can be seen above to the west. This massive outcropping is popular with technical rock climbers and you may see a roped party slowly working their way up the incline.

Begin a series of short switchbacks and continue climbing steeply to a viewpoint at 1.1 miles. Turn left (southeast), descend steeply for 150 yards, then resume climbing. A few times the route goes between or over small boulders and occasionally the grade is level. Along this section you wil be able to look down onto much of Boulder. Wind up the final 0.1 mile to a point directly below the Royal Arch. Climb 75 feet along the trail to a fine viewpoint under the Arch.

The Royal Arch

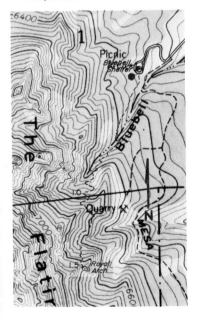

The names and the headquarters address of the national forests, national park and recreation area and city park in northern Colorado relevant to this book and the numbers of the trails that begin in or travel through the specific forests or parks follows:

White River National Forest
Federal Building
Ninth and Grand Avenue
Glenwood Springs, Colorado 81601
    1   2   3   4   5   6

Routt National Forest
P.O. Box 1198
Steamboat Springs, Colorado 80477
    7   8   9   10 11 12 13
    14 15 16 17 18 19 20

Arapaho National Forest
1010 Tenth Street
Golden, Colorado 80401
    20 21 22 23 59 60 61
    62 63 64 65 71 73

Roosevelt National Forest
Rocky Mountain Bank & Trust Bldg.
211 Canyon
Fort Collins, Colorado 80521
    24 25 26 27 50 66 67
    68 69 70 71 72 73 74
    75 76 77 78 79

Shadow Mountain National
    Recreation Area
P.O. Box 1080
Estes Park, Colorado 80517
    28

Rocky Mountain National Park
P.O. Box 1080
Estes Park, Colorado 80517
    29 30 31 32 33 34 35
    36 37 38 39 40 41 42
    43 44 45 46 47 48 49
    51 52 53 54 55 56 57 58

Boulder Mountain Park
Parks and Recreation Department
Box 791
Boulder, Colorado 80302
    80

PHOTO IDENTIFICATION:

Page   3 — The Flatirons,
            Boulder Mountain Park

Page   4 — Grassy Pass,
            Rawah Wilderness

Page 174 — Abandoned buildings
            near Moffat Tunnel

Page 176 — Tarn below Crystal Lake,
            Rocky Mountain National Park